Errata

Pages 6 and 163 contain illegible material. Illustrations 1.2 and 13.11 are more clearly reproduced here.

Illustration 1.2
Searching for Information on the Information Age: Getting Started

To demonstrate the power and efficiency of information searching and retrieval by means of online computer systems, we conducted a small search for published materials on "the information age," using Dialog Information Systems (tm) as the vendor. A summary of what we did and what we got for our efforts is shown below and on Illustration 1.3. The search involved three steps:

1. Identifying the best data bank to search;

2. Searching the selected data bank for relevant reference citations;

3. Looking at a few illustrative "hits" to ensure that we found what we want. (Printing all of them would normally be the next step.)

For the first step, we used Dialog's File 411, which allows the searcher to ascertain at very low cost, the number of reference citations held by different data banks on a specific topic. Rather than specify individual data banks on our own, we chose to use two preselected sets of data banks having to do with <u>information science</u> and with <u>business management</u>, asking for a count of items with either "information age" or "information era" (another commonly used term) in the title, abstract, or list of descriptors.

The results looked like this:

```
File 411:DIALINDEX(tm)
     (Copr. DIALOG Inf.Ser.Inc.)
* New categories will be effective Feb 1.
?SF BUSTEXT, INFOSCI
File  15: ABI/INFORM - 71-88/Feb. WEEK 1
File  49: Pais International - 76-87/Dec
File  75: MANAGEMENT CONTENTS - 74-88/JAN
File  90: FOREIGN TRADE & ECON ABSTRACTS - 74-88/FEB
File 122: Harvard Business Review -- 1971-87,Nov/Dec
File 139: ECONOMIC LITERATURE INDEX - 1969-87/SEP
File 148: TRADE AND INDUSTRY INDEX 81-88/JAN
File 151: Health Planning and Administration - 1975-88/Mar
File 189: Industry Data Sources 79-87/OCT
File 268: FINIS: FINANCIAL INDUSTRY INFORMATION
File   1: ERIC - 66-87/DEC                              1: ERIC - 66-87/DEC
File   6: NTIS - 64-88/ISS04                               101199  INFORMATION
File  12: INSPEC - 1969 thru 1976                            1924  ERA?
File  13: INSPEC - 77-88/ISS04                              66683  AGE?
File  61: LISA - 69-87 (8712)                                 362  INFORMATION(W)(ERA? OR AGE?)
File 202: INFORMATION SCIENCE ABSTRACTS 66-87/JUL
                                                        6: NTIS - 64-88/ISS04
File        Items  Description                             191255  INFORMATION
----        -----  -----------                             180960  ERA?
?SS INFORMATION(W)(ERA? OR AGE?)                            66444  AGE?
                                                              292  INFORMATION(W)(ERA? OR AGE?)
 15: ABI/INFORM - 71-88/Feb, WEEK 1
       58517  INFORMATION                                12: INSPEC - 1969 thru 1976
        2657  ERA?                                          45545  INFORMATION
       40698  AGE?                                           1235  ERA?
         287  INFORMATION(W)(ERA? OR AGE?)                   9117  AGE?
                                                               30  INFORMATION(W)(ERA? OR AGE?)
 49: Pais International - 76-87/Dec
        6916  INFORMATION                                13: INSPEC - 77-88/ISS04
         603  ERA?                                         122295  INFORMATION
        7909  AGE?                                           4311  ERA?
          41  INFORMATION(W)(ERA? OR AGE?)                  26758  AGE?
                                                              749  INFORMATION(W)(ERA? OR AGE?)
 75: MANAGEMENT CONTENTS - 74-88/JAN
       19262  INFORMATION                                61: LISA - 69-87 (8712)
         822  ERA?                                          41386  INFORMATION
       17505  AGE?                                            299  ERA?
          78  INFORMATION(W)(ERA? OR AGE?)                   3216  AGE?
                                                              185  INFORMATION(W)(ERA? OR AGE?)
 90: FOREIGN TRADE & ECON ABSTRACTS - 74-88/FEB
        7797  INFORMATION                                202: INFORMATION SCIENCE ABSTRACTS 66-87/JUL
         389  ERA?                                         104909  INFORMATION
        4286  AGE?                                            648  ERA?
          22  INFORMATION(W)(ERA? OR AGE?)                   4805  AGE?
                                                              245  INFORMATION(W)(ERA? OR AGE?)
```

Information
and the Future

A Handbook of Sources and Strategies

ALICE CHAMBERS WYGANT

AND

O. W. MARKLEY

Greenwood Press

New York • Westport, Connecticut • London

Library of Congress Cataloging-in-Publication Data

Wygant, Alice Chambers, 1948–
    Information and the future : a handbook of sources and strategies /
    Alice Chambers Wygant and O. W. Markley.
        p. cm.
    Bibliography: p.
    Includes index.
    ISBN 0–313–24813–3 (lib. bdg. : alk. paper)
    1. Forecasting—Information services—Handbooks, manuals, etc.
2. Forecasting—Research—Handbooks, manuals, etc. 3. Forecasting —
Bibliography—Handbooks, manuals, etc. 4. Reference books—
Forecasting—Bibliography—Handbooks, manuals, etc. I. Markley,
O. W. II. Title.
CB158.W94 1988
303.4'9'072—dc 19   87–36063

British Library Cataloguing in Publication is available.

Library of Congress Catalog Card Number: 87–36063
ISBN: 0–313–24813–3

First Published in 1988

Greenwood Press, Inc.
88 Post Road West, Westport, Connecticut 06881

Printed in the United States of America

∞™

The paper used in this book complies with the
Permanent Paper Standard issued by the National
Information Standards Organization (Z39.48–1984).

10 9 8 7 6 5 4 3 2 1

Contents

Illustrations

Preface and Acknowledgments

Ever since 1970, when Alvin Toffler coined the term *Future Shock*, it has been commonplace to observe that the pace of change in society is accelerating. And with the "microchip" and other new technologies that have continued to evolve since that time, there is no end in sight.

Less commonplace is the recognition that continuing social change makes it quite difficult to *influence* social change for the better—rather than the worse—if for no reason other than that it's harder to hit the bull's eye on a moving target than on a stationary one, especially a target that has significantly changed its shape from that we learned about in school. With things having become so turbulent and complex, it is difficult to learn what we need to know to make wise decisions before our newly found knowledge has itself become obsolete. The problem is aptly caught by the titles of two works which significantly influenced the thinking that resulted in this handbook: FREEDOM IN A ROCKING BOAT: CHANGING VALUES IN AN UNSTABLE SOCIETY by Sir Geoffrey Vickers (London: Penguin, 1970); and ON LEARNING TO PLAN—AND PLANNING TO LEARN: THE SOCIAL PSYCHOLOGY OF CHANGING TOWARD FUTURE-RESPONSIVE SOCIETAL LEARNING by D. Michael (San Francisco: Jossey-Bass, 1973).

The writing of this handbook was in large part undertaken because a decade-long search for a single book, series of books, or other unitary materials on how the major societal and ecological systems act, interact, and are influenced through the policy process, had to be given up. They do not exist, and probably cannot be written in such a way as would enable forecasters, planners, and leaders to take these factors adequately into account as they try to accurately reflect changing trends, trend discontinuities, and emerging events of various kinds in their work. In spite of such prodigious efforts as James Miller's magnum opus, LIVING SYSTEMS (New York: McGraw Hill, 1977), the foreseeable state of the art is such that if there were a body of writing having this purpose, it would be so enormous and complex that it would not be practicable to commit to writing; and if it were trivialized, it would inevitably lead to trouble-making oversimplifications, such as those which frequently occur when bureaucratic administrators make "change management" decisions without considering important interactions and higher-order impacts that will surely occur when their decisions are implemented.

The driving motivation which ultimately led to the writing of this handbook thus became a more modest one: to learn how to quickly and systematically gather *"situationally relevant strategic information"*—i.e., whatever information may turn out to be needed in order to understand just enough about *those parts of "the system" with which one needs to interact*—so as to enable the making of good decisions as to how best to proceed, whatever your purposes are.

This second pursuit was made immeasurably easier by "cross-fertilizing" the professional knowledge of reference librarians with that of futures researchers and professional lobbyists; and unlike the first task, it was successful enough that the writing of this handbook seemed appropriate. Inasmuch as a number of people were involved at various stages, it is only fitting to mention at least those who led in the making of key turns in the path. There are many more who helped at each stage who are not mentioned by name.

The first of these "fellow travelers" was Myra Hodgson, then a research assistant to O. W. Markley at the Stanford Research Institute. In 1975 she took on the task of learning what reference librarians know and how this could be applied to the task of doing literature research for futures researchers at SRI's Center for the Study of Social Policy. Her specific assignment was to figure out how, when doing literature research on various topics related to "alternative futures" research, it would be possible to avoid getting either one or two books on the one hand, or a wheelbarrow load on the other, but no happy medium in between—which at the time was a truly significant problem for the team.

A second turning point came in 1982 when Tina Byrne, an instructor for the Dialog Information Systems' Houston office, gave an invited introductory presentation on online searching to a futures research class at the University of Houston-Clear Lake. In it, she contrasted the characteristics between a precision and an exhaustive search, and demonstrated how to "cascade" a number of searches on a given topic (for example, regional water quality and availability) across different data bases in order to systematically tap information on different facets of the issue area—an insight which responded directly to the concern noted above.

Things moved ahead much further in 1983 when Alice Wygant, herself a reference librarian, undertook the writing of A GUIDE TO THE LIBRARY FOR STUDENTS OF FUTURES STUDIES as her final project for the M.S. in Studies of the Future at UH-Clear Lake. In it, Ms. Wygant showed that there were specific methods and sources for future-oriented information searching that differed from conventional literature research, and that they could be conveyed in an efficient way to students. This handbook is in part an expansion of that report.

During this same period, Paula Bidlake, now also a graduate of the UH-Clear Lake Studies of the Future Program, began helping O. W. Markley derive the principal ways in which future-oriented information searching, environmental scanning, forecasting, and strategic planning activities might be integrated with the types of inquiry that lobbyists and other political activists make as they seek to influence the systems of society of greatest concern to them.

Finally, acknowledgment is also gratefully given to the "Futures" faculty and graduate students at UH-Clear Lake, many of whom pilot-tested the concepts and reference information presented herein, and to other colleagues who made useful comments on the final draft.

PART I

ACCESS

1

Introduction: What This Book Is All About

Ours is a data-rich and information-poor society...Although the body of science and technology and the population of the world have both grown exponentially in the last two hundred and fifty years, wisdom, perception, and other individual traits have not.

—Martin Shubik

To share what he learned from teaching future studies a professor told the following ancient Chinese parable:

An old man lived with his son in an ancient unused fort on a hill. One day his horse, on which he depended, strayed and was lost. His neighbors came and sympathized with him on his bad luck.

"How do you know this is bad luck?" he asked. Some days later his horse appeared, together with some wild horses, which the man and his son trained. The neighbors this time congratulated him on his good luck.

"How do you know this is good luck?" asked the old man. As it happened his son, while riding one of the horses, was thrown and became permanently lame. His neighbors consoled him and again spoke of his ill luck.

"How do you know this is ill luck?" he asked.

Not long after war broke out and the son, because of his lameness, could not go.

This parable has been attributed to Lao-tsu, a Chinese philosopher who founded Taoism in the first century B.C. It was quoted by Basil McDermott in "What Ten Years of Teaching the Future Has Taught Me" (in EDU-

CATIONAL FUTURES: SOURCEBOOK I, edited by Fred Kierstead, Jim Bowman, and Chris Dede. Washington, D.C.: World Future Society, 1979. Pages 220–234).

The story of the old man teaches different lessons on many levels. For our purposes the moral of the story is to never form knee-jerk, or premature judgements about the future. Although there is much we cannot control, and although we may not understand the ultimate consequences of our actions, there is much that we can learn if we know where to look.

Information and the Future

There are three fundamentally different ways of dealing with the future. Most frequently, people ignore it, acting as though the future will be enough like the past that existing knowledge and habitual methods will suffice. Although we must use this approach in most aspects of our lives, it can lead to trouble when we ignore changes of importance that might have been foreseen.

A second approach is to look at how things are changing; to develop a sense of foresight about how the future is likely to differ from the past; and how we may need to change what we do to fit with it. Although this approach makes it possible to minimize the troublesome "crisis reaction" style of management encountered so frequently in changing times, it doesn't necessarily steer us in the direction we need to go to achieve our aspirations. A third approach, therefore, is to envision those things we wish to achieve or create, as well as those we wish to avoid or eliminate.

As Illustration 1.1 indicates, these may be thought of as the reactive, responsive, and creative strategies. While the creative strategy is necessary in order to deliberately shape the future, the responsive strategy is frequently necessary to influence things successfully. The reactive strategy also influences the future if only by default. Thus, although people usually don't think of it this way, most of what we do influences the future in one way or another, and our abilities to achieve our objectives can be significantly strengthened by knowing how to find and use relevant information—especially in changing times. This is particularly true of students, journalists, or other researchers who want to find an introductory article, a review of the literature, or bibliographic citations covering an unfamiliar topic.

Strategic planners, forecasters, and analysts want better information on markets, competitors, new technologies or other factors that might influence their long-term or immediate future. Lobbyists, as well as issues management specialists, and other concerned citizens want to know how to better argue their cases, and to effectively forge coalitions in support of them. This handbook is designed to help all types of readers to carry out custom-made searches for the information they need, and to apply that information to their situation.

Illustration 1.1
Three Ways to Influence the Future

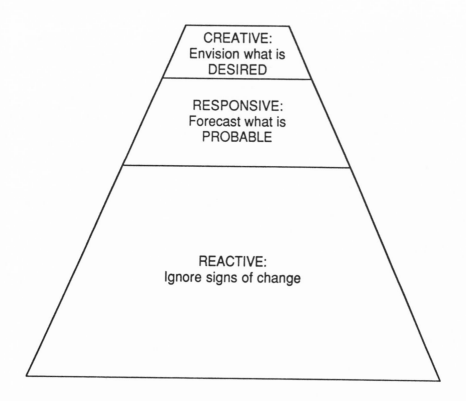

CREATIVE:
Envision what is
DESIRED

RESPONSIVE:
Forecast what is
PROBABLE

REACTIVE:
Ignore signs of change

Access to Information in the Information Age

Access to relevant information has always been important to those who influence their world consistently and successfully. But only recently has information access become an important field in its own right. Hundreds of databanks storing up-to-date information now exist for public use, each focusing on a specific topic such as education, ecology, or the future. Microcomputers can be used at home, at the office, or in libraries to gain "online" access to this important source of information by means of telephone "modem" connection to commercial access companies that have standardized the process for searching different databanks.

Illustrations 1.2 and 1.3 show how online searches can be done quickly and inexpensively.

Illustration 1.2
Searching for Information on the Information Age: Getting Started

To demonstrate the power and efficiency of information searching and retrieval by means on online computer systems, we conducted a small search for published materials on "the information age," using Dialog Information Systems (tm) as the vendor. A summary of what we did and what we got for our efforts is shown below, and on Illustration 1.3. The search involved three steps:

1. Identifying the best data bank to search;

2. Searching the selected data bank for relevant reference citations;

3. Looking at a few illustrative "hits" and choosing the output through which to have the findings retrieved—either online through our own computer terminal, or printed offline by the vendor at a lower cost and sent to us by mail the following day.

For the first step, we used Dialog's File 411, which allows the searcher to ascertain at very low cost, the number of reference citations held by different data banks on a specific topic. Rather than specify individual data banks on our own, however, w chose to look at preselected groups of data banks having to do with information science and with business management, asking for a frequency count of bibliographical items contained in each data bank searched that happen to have either "information age" or "information era" (another commonly used term) in its title, its abstract, or its list of descriptors.

The results looked like this:

```
File 411:DIALINDEX(tm)
        (Copr. DIALOG Inf.Ser.Inc.)
# New categories will be effective Feb 1.
?SF BUSIEXT, INFOSCI
File  15: ABI/INFORM - 71-88/Feb, WEEK 1
File  49: Pais International - 76-87/Dec
File  75: MANAGEMENT CONTENTS - 74-88/JAN
File  90: FOREIGN TRADE & ECON ABSTRACTS - 74-88/FEB
File 122: Harvard Business Review -- 1971-87,Nov/Dec
File 139: ECONOMIC LITERATURE INDEX - 1969-87/SEP
File 148: TRADE AND INDUSTRY INDEX 81-88/JAN
File 151: Health Planning and Administration - 1975-88/Mar
File 189: Industry Data Sources 79-87/OCT
File 266: FINIS: FINANCIAL INDUSTRY INFORMATION
File   1: ERIC - 66-87/DEC
File   6: NTIS - 64-88/ISS04
File  12: INSPEC - 1969 thru 1976
File  13: INSPEC - 77-88/ISS04
File  61: LISA - 69-87 (8712)
File 202: INFORMATION SCIENCE ABSTRACTS 66-87/JUL

File      Items  Description
----      -----  -----------

?SS INFORMATION(W)(ERA? OR AGE?)

15: ABI/INFORM - 71-88/Feb, WEEK 1
      58517  INFORMATION
       2457  ERA?
      40698  AGE?
        297  INFORMATION(W)(ERA? OR AGE?)

49: Pais International - 76-87/Dec
       6916  INFORMATION
        603  ERA?
       7809  AGE?
         41  INFORMATION(W)(ERA? OR AGE?)

75: MANAGEMENT CONTENTS - 74-88/JAN
      19262  INFORMATION
        822  ERA?
      17505  AGE?
         78  INFORMATION(W)(ERA? OR AGE?)

90: FOREIGN TRADE & ECON ABSTRACTS - 74-88/FEB
       7797  INFORMATION
        389  ERA?
       4286  AGE?
         22  INFORMATION(W)(ERA? OR AGE?)
```

```
122: Harvard Business Review -- 1971-87,Nov/Dec
       1016  INFORMATION
        156  ERA?
        806  AGE?
         12  INFORMATION(W)(ERA? OR AGE?)

1: ERIC - 66-87/DEC
     101199  INFORMATION
       1924  ERA?
      66683  AGE?
        362  INFORMATION(W)(ERA? OR AGE?)

6: NTIS - 64-88/ISS04
     191255  INFORMATION
     180960  ERA?
      66444  AGE?
        292  INFORMATION(W)(ERA? OR AGE?)

12: INSPEC - 1969 thru 1976
      45545  INFORMATION
       1235  ERA?
       9117  AGE?
         30  INFORMATION(W)(ERA? OR AGE?)

13: INSPEC - 77-88/ISS04
     122295  INFORMATION
       4311  ERA?
      26758  AGE?
        749  INFORMATION(W)(ERA? OR AGE?)

61: LISA - 69-87 (8712)
      41386  INFORMATION
        299  ERA?
       3216  AGE?
        185  INFORMATION(W)(ERA? OR AGE?)

202: INFORMATION SCIENCE ABSTRACTS 66-87/JUL
     104909  INFORMATION
        648  ERA?
       4805  AGE?
        245  INFORMATION(W)(ERA? OR AGE?)
```

With high-speed telecommunications, it is possible to immediately "download" online files to a microcomputer rather than sending for printed "hard copy." Moreover, the software now exists to allow users to re-search such files in their own computer using powerful search commands like those used by the commercial vendor's software.

These few illustrations only scratch the surface of new information technologies already available. Even more dazzling possibilities are expected in

Illustration 1.3
Searching for Information on the Information Age: Getting Results

Next, we chose to search the data bank called ABI/INFORM (Dialog File No. 15). We chose it because it is a repository for management-oriented materials, rather than those having a more technical orientation, even though it was not the data bank having the greatest number of "hits." And because it had many more citations than we would want to look at, we focused the search more tightly by requiring that the search terms be found in the title, rather than elsewhere.

The results are shown below in several different "formats" (item number and title only; full reference citation; and bibliographic information only).

```
File  15:ABI/INFORM - 71-88/JAN, WEEK 4
        (Copr. UMI/Data Courier  1988)

      Set  Items  Description
      ---  -----  -----------
?ss information(w)(era? or age?)

      S1   58374  INFORMATION
      S2    2649  ERA?
      S3   40607  AGE?
      S4     286  INFORMATION(W)(ERA? OR AGE?)
?s s4/ti

      S5     107  S4/TI


?t5/6/1-10



  5/6/1
88002328
   Desk Jobs: Marketing the Information Age


  5/6/2
88001507
   The Challenge of the New Information Age


  5/6/3
88001490
   The Data PBX: The Darling of the Information Age


  5/6/4
87040064
   Information  Age  Calls  for  New  Methods  of  Financial  Analysis  in
Implementing Manufacturing Technologies


  5/6/5
87034266


  5/6/6
87033750
   Managing  Our  Professional  Integrity and Competence in the Information
Age


  5/6/7
87032978
   Demands  of  Information  Age  Set Pace for Publishing-Related Machinery
Industry
```

Illustration 1.3—Continued

t5/5/1-5

5/5/1
88002328
  Desk Jobs: Marketing the Information Age
  Gordon, Jack
  Training v24n12 PP: 37-43 Dec 1987 CODEN: TRNGB6 ISSN: 0095-5892
JRNL CODE: TBI
  DOC TYPE: Journal Paper LANGUAGE: English LENGTH: 7 Pages
  AVAILABILITY: ABI/INFORM

The US transition to an information society has been made more
dramatic, uncertain, and urgent by the rapid acceleration of technological
change. A definitive picture of the nature of work in 10 or 15 years is not
yet attainable. Debate continues over whether the new technological tools
will actually "skill up" jobs by making them more interesting and much more
demanding, or whether technology will "skill down" jobs so that workers
function as mere attendants to machines. Technology is transforming US
workers' jobs into desk jobs with a conceptual focus. However, Karl
Albrecht, an author and consultant, postulates that only about 15% of
workers are really "thinkers," while the remainder are "doers." Critical to
workers' transition to jobs in the information society will be the ability
to educate and socialize "laborers" regarding the actual value of
electronic paperwork as work. Perhaps, the glamour and excitement being
attributed to business today is part of an attempt to market desk jobs.
  DESCRIPTORS: Clerical personnel; White collar workers; Blue collar
workers; Trends; Employee attitude (PER); Job attitudes; Technological
change; Impacts; Effects; Job satisfaction
  CLASSIFICATION CODES: 2500 (CN=Organizational behavior)

5/5/2
88001507
  The Challenge of the New Information Age
  Oguchi, Bun-Ichi
  Telephone Engineer & Mgmt v91n23(Part 2) PP: 4-5 Dec 1, 1987 CODEN:
TPEMAW ISSN: 0040-263X JRNL CODE: TEM
  DOC TYPE: Journal Paper LANGUAGE: English LENGTH: 2 Pages
  AVAILABILITY: ABI/INFORM

Extensions of original voice and computer data communication services
are quickly moving society into a new information age. Fujitsu Ltd. is at
the forefront of creating advanced communication systems and equipment for
today's advanced information requirements. These products include public
and corporate network systems and equipment for optical, satellite, and
microwave communications. In Japan, Fujitsu has created a private
integrated services digital network (ISDN) called Corporate Information
Network System. The system uses high-speed digital leased lines to
integrate individual networks into multimedia networks. The company has
taken an innovative approach to hardware development in order to continue
to meet evolving requirements of ISDN hardware components. Its goal is to
develop hardware with sufficient flexibility and expandability to meet
future demand for advanced telecommunication services. Fujitsu also has
developed 2 kinds of earth stations for Japan's satellite communications.
  COMPANY NAMES: Fujitsu Ltd (DUNS 69-053-5281)
  DESCRIPTORS: Communications systems; ISDN; Standards; Technology; Case
studies; Electronics industry
  CLASSIFICATION CODES: 8650 (CN=Electrical & electronics industries);

Illustration 1.3—Continued

t5/3/1-10

5/3/1
88002328
   Desk Jobs: Marketing the Information Age
   Gordon, Jack
   Training v24n12 PP: 37-43 Dec 1987
   AVAILABILITY: ABI/INFORM

5/3/2
88001507
   The Challenge of the New Information Age
   Oguchi, Bun-Ichi
   Telephone Engineer & Mgmt v91n23(Part 2) PP: 4-5 Dec 1, 1987
   AVAILABILITY: ABI/INFORM

5/3/3
88001490
   The Data PBX: The Darling of the Information Age
   Chewning, Steve
   Telephony v213n23 PP: 46-47 Dec 7, 1987
   AVAILABILITY: ABI/INFORM

5/3/4
87040064
   Information Age Calls for New Methods of Financial Analysis in
Implementing Manufacturing Technologies
   O'Guin, Michael C.
   Industrial Engineering v19n11 PP: 36-40 Nov 1987
   AVAILABILITY: ABI/INFORM

5/3/5
87034266
   Broadband Packet Switching: The Network Enters the Information Age
   Decina, Maurizio
   Telecommunications v21n9(North American Edition) PP: 98,101 Sep 1987
   AVAILABILITY: ABI/INFORM

5/3/6
87033750
   Managing Our Professional Integrity and Competence in the Information
Age
   Morse, Herbert E.; Schmitz, Clarence T.
   Ohio CPA Jrnl v46n3 PP: 5-7 Summer 1987
   AVAILABILITY: ABI/INFORM

5/3/7
87032978
   Demands of Information Age Set Pace for Publishing-Related Machinery
Industry
   Nomoto, Fukashi
   Business Japan (Japan) v32n4 PP: 51,53 Apr 1987

the near future. For example, a new field called "knowledge engineering" translates human expertise into a form that can be imitated by artificial intelligence. This translation is necessary so that the computerized "expert system" can efficiently and effectively replace the human expert in repetitive tasks that use the same type of judgement each time.

Expert systems will probably be available within a few years to conduct many of the types of information searches described in this handbook in an automated or semi-automated fashion. Moreover, knowledge engineering may one day become so automated that computers will identify, retrieve, and synthesize needed information from integrated networks of data covering diverse disciplines.

Not surprisingly then, one often hears of an emerging "information industry." The information industry is not really a new concept. Several books written in the sixties and seventies defined it and predicted the enormous influence it would have on society. Two seminal works were THE PRODUCTION AND DISTRIBUTION OF KNOWLEDGE by Fritz Machlup (Princeton, N.J.: Princeton University Press, 1962) and THE INFORMATION SECTOR: DEFINITION AND MEASUREMENT, a doctoral dissertation by Marc Porat (Stanford, Calif.: Stanford University, 1976).

Two subsequent, popular authors, Alvin Toffler in THE THIRD WAVE (New York: Morrow, 1980) and John Naisbitt in MEGATRENDS: TEN NEW DIRECTIONS TRANSFORMING OUR LIVES (6th ed., New York: Warner Books, 1983) have popularized the view that the structure of our society is being transformed by the new information industry. Less well known, but no less important was INFORMATION SERVICES: ECONOMICS, MANAGEMENT, AND TECHNOLOGY (edited by Robert M. Mason and John E. Creps, Jr., Boulder, Col.: Westview Press, 1980).

These authors predict that just as the agricultural age gave way to an industrial age over the past several centuries, the industrial age is now giving way to an information age. Because this transition is expected to occur in the space of several decades rather than several centuries, the management and planning leaders of tomorrow will be those who learn to gather and process information quickly.

The Chinese character for "crisis," which combines both the symbol for "danger" and that for "opportunity" is a good metaphor for the transition from the industrial to the information age. A society in transition is more open to manipulative influence than is a static society; and it seems obvious that like all tools, information technology will frequently be used to create advantage for some but disadvantage for many others. The development of human moral and ethical maturity over centuries has not kept pace with technological advancement.

Thus, in addition to helping persons and organizations use the new information technologies for self-serving ends, an important purpose of this handbook is to help researchers, planners, and community leaders use these powerful new information tools for the common good as well; working toward a society that is both sustainable and humane in spite of the many emerging threats to our collective quality of life.

Access to Information for Influencing the Future

People who are new either to the art of systematic information searching or to the art of planning often find it quite uncomfortable to confront the bewildering array of possible questions and available information sources that might be explored. Thus it is helpful to researchers to have a good checklist or two for purposes of envisioning what it is that they want to ask for, and for guiding them through the process.

One such "guidelist" is the twelve-step Guided Design Process summarized in Illustration 1.4. It was developed to teach problem solving and decision making in college courses using a strategy called "Guided Design." More information about books on teaching decision making and a free movie on Guided Design are available from the Center for Guided Design (P.O. Box 6101, West Virginia University, Morgantown, WV 26506–6101. 304/293–3445).

A second checklist is presented in Illustration 1.5. It contains a simplified list of planning questions which help the user to be more future-oriented than the steps of the Guided Design Process.

Overview of this Handbook

Part I, Access, is a beginner's introduction to information acquisition. In Chapter 1, Introduction, we state our assumptions about the mission, objectives, and intended audience of the book, and provide guidelines to help different types of readers adapt this handbook to their personal needs.

In Chapter 2, Designing the Information Search Process, we introduce the various information search strategies available today. For students getting started on a research paper, or readers with little experience in information searching, this may be the most useful chapter of the handbook.

Part II, Sources, introduces various sources currently available for searches of published and unpublished information. This is a detailed directory of the major information sources and how to use them. It is to be used for reference purposes, and is written as an annotated guide for beginners and experts alike. Part II also presents practical applications of the theories presented in Part I.

Part III, Applications, introduces advanced strategies for influencing the future through the skillful use of information. It introduces methods and tools that have widespread application to business, government, and the voluntary sectors of society. Chapter 12, Information and Social Change, introduces two process maps which facilitate future-oriented information

Illustration 1.4
The Decision-Making Process Used in Guided Design

DEFINE THE SITUATION

‡   Observe or visualize the situation that exists and analyze to define what is, in terms of the actors, props, action, scene, cause, and consequences.

STATE THE GOAL

1.   Identify Situation Problems   Analyze to define what it is about the consequences of the situation that might be, contribute to, or cause a problem.

2.   Create Goal Options   Imagine what could be and generate goal options that solve each problem. Integrate ideas and synthesize goal statements.

3.   Select the Goal   Specify musts and wants, constraints and assumptions, anticipate future consequences, evaluate, and select the best goal.

GENERATE IDEAS

4.   Identify Goal Problems   Analyze to define what it is that might be, contribute to, or cause a problem if the goal is to be achieved.

5.   Create Idea Options   Imagine what could be and generate idea options that solve each problem. Integrate ideas and synthesize combinations.

6.   Select Ideas   Consider the goal, specify additional constraints and assumptions, anticipate future consequences, evaluate, and select the best combination of ideas.

DEFINE THE NEW SITUATION

‡‡   Visualize the situation that results if the selected ideas are implemented and analyze to define what may be, in terms of the actors, props, action, scene, cause, consequences plus any construction, operation, and the cost/benefits.

PREPARE A PLAN

7.   Identify New Situation Problems   Analyze to define what it is about the new situation that might be, contribute to or cause a problem.

8.   Create Plan Options   Imagine what could be and generate plan options that solve each problem. Integrate ideas and synthesize detailed plans.

9.   Select A Plan   Consider the goal, selected ideas, the constraints and assumptions, and anticipate future consequences. Evaluate and select the best plan.

TAKE ACTION

10.   Identify Plan Problems   Visualize or rehearse the plan. Analyze to define what it is that might be, contribute to or cause a problem when the plan is implemented.

11.   Create Action Options   Physically implement the plan. Imagine what could be, and generate action options that solve each problem that occurs.

12.   Select the Next Action   Compare the results of the action with the goal, the selected ideas, and the plan. Specify constraints and assumptions, anticipate future consequences, evaluate, and select the best future action.

Source: C. E. Wales, A. H. Nardi, and R. A. Stager. *Professional Decision-Making*, Center for Guided Design, West Virginia University, 1986.

Illustration 1.5
A Basic Checklist of Planning Questions

1. What are my (or my group's) predominant $\left\{\begin{array}{l}\text{hopes}\\\text{fears}\\\text{expectations}\end{array}\right\}$

   for the future?

2. What do I (we) particularly want to $\left\{\begin{array}{l}\text{protect}\\\text{maintain}\\\text{achieve}\\\text{change}\\\text{create}\end{array}\right\}$ in

   the $\left\{\begin{array}{l}\text{short}\\\text{medium}\\\text{long}\end{array}\right\}$ range?

3. What are the $\left\{\begin{array}{l}\text{strengths}\\\text{weaknesses}\\\text{opportunities}\\\text{threats}\\\text{other factors}\end{array}\right\}$ that need to be

   considered? In particular, what obstacles would prevent
   success if not changed or otherwise overcome?

4. How, and with whom, do I want to "plan for action?"

5. What methods, tools, or strategies look most promising?

6. How much time and effort am I (and others I can count on)
   willing to exert on this, and for how long? What other
   resources are likely to be available?

7. Assuming that adequate time and effort is expended to
   implement the plans within whatever resource constraints are
   likely, what outcomes are realistic to expect, and when?

8. Given whatever answers you have to the above questions, is
   the venture really worth doing? If so, who should do what?
   When? What are the first steps?

searching: the Strategic Intelligence Cycle and the Issue Emergence Cycle. The former highlights what information to look for and how to use what is found; the latter highlights specific information sources useful at various stages in the life of a public policy issue.

Chapter 12 also lists four basic methodologies for translating information into strategic action:

1. Environmental intelligence and strategic assessment.

2. Strategic forecasting and scenario development.

3. Strategic planning and policy development.
4. Human and organization development.

Chapter 13, The Future of Economic Development and Quality of Life in Yourtown: A Scenario, illustrates how multiple searches can be custom-fit to the needs of a given client or problem. The principles presented throughout this handbook are integrated into a scenario in which a team of researchers, planners, and concerned citizens from a hypothetical community, Yourtown, garner the information needed to promote economic growth and quality of life in their region.

Finally, Chapter 14, Parting Tips, closes with a few caveats and suggestions often left out of technical reference books. These tips are usually learned the hard way, through bitter experience.

Part IV, Appendixes, concludes the book with some supplementary material too lengthy and tangential for the main body of the text.

How to Use this Handbook

People who will find this handbook useful include high school and college students, teachers and professors, forecasters, strategic planners, professional analysts, lobbyists, networkers, concerned citizens, journalists, and reference librarians. With such a diverse audience in mind, we designed the handbook to be used in any of three different ways:

1. For those who want to become proficient at information searching and research in their own right, we suggest that it be used as a text book: first, by reading it straight through and then by using it as a reference book as needed for specific types of information.
2. Reference librarians and other professional researchers already familiar with much of this material themselves may want to use the book as a teaching tool to explain different search processes to their patrons.
3. For those planning to hire professional searchers, this handbook is a way to learn the basic principles of searching quickly, and its primary tools. With this knowledge, the client can specify precisely the services needed.

For college-level classes which include a one- to three-week assignment on information searching, the handbook can be used as either a textbook or a reference guide. It was successfully pilot-tested for this purpose in a business school course on strategic planning and management policy, as well as in conventional research methods courses.

On the Obsolescence of this Handbook and Other Caveats

A guidebook to any field that is changing as fast as the information field is bound to be somewhat out of date, even before it is published. This handbook is no exception. However, many basic research techniques are relatively unchanging.

The main purpose of this handbook is not so much to point researchers to specific sources as to teach them how to find the sources they need when they need them. As the Chinese philosopher observed in the KUAN-TZU, a 4th century B.C. book of philosophy:

> If you give a man a fish,
> He will have a single meal,
> If you teach him how to fish,
> He will eat all his life.

Although the information field itself will be undergoing a number of changes with the advent of new search tools, the research methods taught in this handbook will maintain validity and will even help researchers stay abreast of new developments in the field.

By way of concluding this introduction and partial guide, we wish all our readers GOOD ACCESS!

2

Designing the Information Search Process

Most people seeking information tend to jump immediately into an unfocused search using "piece meal" or "hit and miss" search tactics without trying to systematically analyze their search. Information professionals such as reference librarians have a different approach to this process. They have found that spending some time at the beginning of a search organizing and designing a search strategy makes for a much more productive and efficient search. This chapter tells how to analyze information needs and how to design an information search.

The importance of having a search plan or strategy cannot be overemphasized. There are so many bibliographic tools, both online and in print, to choose from, that without a preconceived plan the searcher ends up floundering and perhaps drowning in the sea of information. In addition, the danger exists that the novice searcher will assume that the information found is all that is available. In reality a skilled researcher who systematically combs the information resources can usually find much more material than the novice. Ill-chosen resources may represent only one aspect of a subject or one side of a controversy. Using a systematic search strategy helps the researcher to cover all the different facets of the subject.

Having a search strategy doesn't mean that the search process is rigid. In fact, quite the contrary, a search strategy helps the process to be dynamic and very responsive to change. Part of any good strategy is the ability to make directional decisions based on the interim results of the search process. It is just as damaging to get into a searching rut such as using only one resource or one particular technique for all information searching as it is to do a "hit and miss" search. The purpose of this book is to explain the kinds of searches professionals do and the resources they use in doing them. These professional searching techniques are easily adapted to almost any information-gathering situation and most of the resources are readily available in local libraries. The existence of these techniques and resources is not classified information and yet it has not been widely known in the past by those other than information professionals. INFORMATION AND THE FUTURE draws all this material together in one source in an easy to understand format for the general reader or novice information searcher.

Types of Searches

There are at least five different kinds of searches: exhaustive, precision, pearl growing, snowball, and situational. Each of these has a different purpose but when used singly or in combination they are the foundation of building a search strategy.

The prototype of the exhaustive search is the doctoral dissertation, in which one of the goals is to identify and provide bibliographic citations to all the relevant literature bearing on any given topic. In an exhaustive search the primary focus is on gathering *all* the information. This type of search is not based on a specific number of citations or a certain amount of information but rather on the depth of research the searcher needs. Because exhaustive searches in many fields would yield bibliographies with thousands of citations it is not widely used except for a very specific topic such as the works of a particular author or to research an emerging area of study. The exhaustive search necessarily includes items of peripheral interest as well as those directly related to the topic.

The precision search seeks to identify those few items that are directly on target for the topic being searched without including any material that may be peripherally relevant. In one kind of precision search the searcher knows exactly what is required before the search begins. For example, the researcher could need to know the population of all the cities in a given geographical region or the molecular weight of a particular element. A precision search can also result in a large number of references but still be on a very precise subject such as the testing of drinking water for *E. coli* bacteria. Just as it was in the exhaustive search the number of citations is not relevant; the determining factor is the specificity of the topic. A search can be both exhaustive and precision at the same time.

Pearl growing is a technique to help researchers get started in a field about which they know very little. Just as an oyster begins to create a pearl by adding layers on top of a grain of sand, the searcher can create a fund of information by layering information resources around a kernel of fact. Using whatever facts are available the searcher can usually get a "toe hold" in the literature and then use that information to refine the search strategy and re-enter the literature. For instance, the name of an author could yield a series of articles on a specific topic which could in turn provide the searcher with the controlled vocabulary terms that were used to index that article. These controlled vocabulary terms are simply words that are used to describe a concept for a particular index. They are controlled because all the synonyms for that word are indexed under the same term. A search on an author's name could also provide words from the titles of the author's articles that could be used to restructure the search. The name of a particular journal could lead the searcher to an index where that journal and others on the same subject are indexed. These reconnaissance missions serve as preliminaries for developing or refining the search strategy.

A snowball survey is used when the information needed is too new or too politically sensitive to be available in published form. In this type of search the researcher identifies the experts in a field and contacts them to ask questions. These questions are usually of a general nature such as: "what is important to know about the question?" and "what sources of information would you recommend?" as well as "who else might have information about the subject?" More specific questions may also be appropriate, depending on the nature of the project.

There are several cautionary points regarding the use of the snowball survey. First, the researcher must remember that experts are very busy people who get many requests for information. Therefore it is imperative that the researcher prepare for the interview by reviewing background information and planning questions so that the expert's time is efficiently used. It is also important that the snowball survey be used in a professional manner. Experts should not be troubled for information that is more readily available in a conventional source. Finally, the searcher should be aware of the possibility that the expert may present information that is biased or incorrect. The information obtained using a snowball survey should be verified to the extent possible in some more traditional source or by comparison to the information received from other experts.

The situational search is simply whatever combination of the options described above that makes the most sense in a given situation. It is a type of search that reflects the interplay between the context in which the search is being done and the content of the bibliographic materials which are found through the search process. A situational search is really the weaving together of all of the processes and bibliographic tools that are discussed in this book. There is great skill involved in knowing what process or resource will work the best at a given time in the search. As the search proceeds the specific situation can change making it advisable for searchers to adapt their strategy. Another purpose of this book is to acquaint searchers with a wide variety of information resources so that more appropriate choices can be made in a particular situation.

Defining the Context of a Search

A search strategy is really just a plan for solving a problem. The first step in devising such a plan should be defining the context of the information request. This is most easily done by answering a series of questions.

"What information do you need?" This first question requires that the searcher identify the subject area that is of interest and focus on some background information in order to define the topic of the search. (Chapter 3, Basic Facts for Beginners, and Chapter 4, General Reference Works, can help with getting started in the library, which is usually the best place to begin the search for background information.) This first step is especially important if the searcher is planning to use an information professional to help with the project. It is impossible to communicate a search request to another person if that request is amorphous or ambiguous. Good reference librarians are adept at helping researchers clarify their thoughts into a coherent search request, but time can be saved and the process is easier if this has already been done.

"Why do you want the information?" Answering the second question allows the researcher to define the purpose of the research and limit the number of activities required to accomplish that purpose.

"How is the information to be used?" Determining how the information is to be used helps the researcher to identify the main concepts and to make a priority list of topics and peripheral topics. This list is useful in several ways. It helps to define the search context even further as well as helping with the allocation of resources. Further analysis of the audience for each information request will determine how extensively the topic should be researched and the format for the information that will be most acceptable. One standard procedure is to organize the bibliography into simple conceptual groups each of which begins with a good introductory overview, a good critical review, and a good technical description. These first three citations are then followed by the more comprehensive bibliography. This format is commonly used when one person is doing research for someone else who will use the information; however, its use can be beneficial to almost anyone.

"How much time and money are available?" While this last question is in many ways a "bottom line" issue when designing a search, it should be addressed only after all three other questions have been answered. Without the information gained from the first three questions it is impossible to realistically estimate the time or the money necessary to do an effective search.

Searchers should rest assured that a lack of money does not mean information retrieval failure. In fact many resources are free. Libraries and reference librarians are available in all areas of the country and are extremely helpful to researchers. Indeed, being helpful to those seeking information is a reference librarian's job. There are also many free or inexpensive government documents. (See Chapter 8, Government Documents.) These are available through libraries and various government agencies. (See Chapter 7, Government Agencies and Officials.) In addition, many groups have established free information hotlines and charitable organizations and foundations that furnish support and information for research. (See Chapter 9, Interest Groups and Networks.)

There are also a number of relatively inexpensive options open for researchers. A judicious combination of searching both the print and online sources can be quite reasonable. Having analyzed the problem and compiled a priority list, as outlined above, the researcher is in a much better position to determine the best commitment of limited resources. In some instances the print version of a source is almost as powerful as the computer version online.

When neither money nor time is a constraint, then the researcher should plan to pay for the expert help of a professional information consultant. It is also advisable to let the consultant help to plan the strategy as well as to conduct the research. With unlimited time and money the researcher can also conduct extensive expert interviews and might even travel to special libraries where more relevant bibliographic resources are available. Generally speaking, the more exhaustive a search, the more expensive it is in terms of *both* time and money.

Most information searches fall somewhere between "no money" and "unlimited money." They are usually a combination of all the situations outlined. The same problem can be searched on several levels and during the course of the search may move back and forth from one level to another. Searches are situational from the point of view of resources as well as that of context.

The "80/20 rule" is a practical guideline or rule of thumb for considering costs. In most situations it seems that 80 percent of the useful information is found in the first 20 percent of the time spent. Therefore, as a practical guideline, it is often useful to budget your time that way. Unless the searcher needs something like an exhaustive search, it is better to search for short periods and then use those results to redefine and refine searching concepts.

A basic, brief preliminary search can provide much guidance for realistically estimating the time and money involved in a project. This is extremely difficult to do without a reconnaissance of the information resources available. Even experts are reluctant to guess without some first-hand knowledge of the subject area resources. Beware of so-called experts who do estimate such things off the top of their heads—they are often wrong.

A final caution about the "80/20 rule," researchers should remember that it is just a rule of thumb and situations should be considered on a case-by-

Illustration 2.1
Information Search Cycle

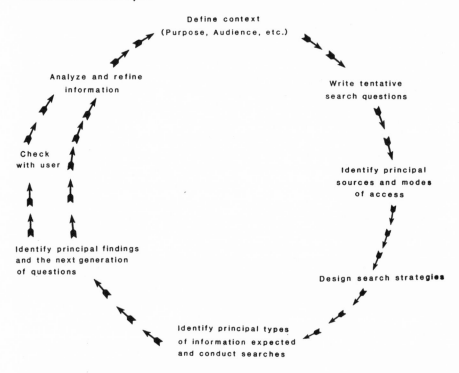

case basis. Also, researchers should remember that the rule itself is just an estimation and is not based on a scientific, rigorous examination of search results.

Information Search Cycle

The Information Search Cycle pictured above shows how a search strategy can be designed using the questions and ideas discussed earlier in this chapter. The strategy can then be used to find information on a given topic. The cyclic design of the information wheel is important because it illustrates the flexibility necessary for good information searching. The researcher must be able to take the information found and analyze it with the idea that the results may necessitate beginning the cycle again.

Worksheet Approach

The worksheet approach is simply another way of analyzing the search process. With the advent of online database searching, information professionals began to reexamine the search process. Many of their conclusions also hold true for any kind of information searching. (See Chapter 6, Online Resources, for a more detailed description of online database searching.) Using a worksheet to define the context of the search and to develop a strategy is an efficient way to get started. The following worksheet is typical of many used by information professionals.

Before beginning to fill in the blank spaces on a worksheet the researcher must determine just why the search is being done. Is it to answer a specific question? Is it to gather information on a certain topic? Is the researcher attempting to make a case for a certain point of view? Once the purpose of the search has been established then a topical sentence can be constructed. This problem statement delineates not only the purpose of the search but the information desired. In other words, what the researcher is trying to find. At this point it is useful to find some background information on the topic to help place the newly found information in the proper context.

The next step is to identify the individual concepts involved in the search. Here the researcher is trying to reduce a narrative sentence to an equation. Once the concepts have been identified then possible information resources can be chosen. Illustration 2.3 is an example of such an equation.

Conclusion

Part II of this book, Sources, is about some of the many resources available. These chapters are also sprinkled with examples to help researchers understand exactly how the tool being discussed could be used in a specific instance. Since each resource may require a slightly different strategy it is necessary to prepare each of the strategies ahead of time. This entails becoming familiar with the controlled vocabulary of descriptive index terms and other bibliographic idiosyncrasies of the individual resources. This is done by analyzing their internal structures in the context of the search being done. Part II gives more detailed information about these sources and how they can be used. Researchers should always have an alternate strategy ready in case the first one doesn't work. "Plan B" should be composed of ways to broaden or narrow the focus of the search as the situation demands.

When the definition of the search is finally complete, the search is executed. The results should be carefully scrutinized with the idea that the strategy can be refined or redefined based on early results.

Ending a search can sometimes be as difficult as beginning one. Because of the cyclical nature of information searching the researcher can continue to redefine and reexecute the search almost indefinitely. If the preliminary planning described earlier in this chapter has been done then the researcher knows what the goals of the search are and when they have been accomplished. There is a fine line between over-searching and appropriate searching. Over-searching is a common problem for novice searchers and especially

Illustration 2.2
Sample Worksheet

TOPIC: (Describe your search topic in one or more
      sentences.)

CONCEPTS: (Divide your search topic as described above into
      its component concepts.)

ALTERNATIVES: (List all the different ways of expressing the
      concepts listed above.)

POSSIBLE SOURCES OF INFORMATION ON SEARCH TOPIC: (List the
      places where your expect to find information.)

CONTROLLED VOCABULARY OR SPECIALIZED STRATEGY: (Translate
      the concepts listed above in the controlled vocabulary
      or strategy most appropriate for the database being
      searched.)

SEARCHING PLAN:

MANUAL   ONLINE   SPECIAL TECHNIQUES

PLAN B: (Alternative strategy to be used if first one does
      not work.)

Illustration 2.3
Information Equation

PROBLEM: Find information about asbestos pollution of
            drinking water.

Concept A	Concept B	Concept C
Asbestos	Pollution	Water

CONCEPT COMBINATION EQUATION

$$A + B + C$$

for those with a sketchy or nonexistent search strategy. The "80/20 rule" discussed earlier in this chapter is helpful to remember at this point.

In Chapter 12, Information and Social Change, an even more advanced set of tools for setting objectives and other aspects of the context for searching is introduced.

PART II

SOURCES

3

Basic Facts for Beginners

There is nothing so captivating as new knowledge.
—Peter Mere Latham

Library organization is based on several interrelated systems. These systems are essential for achieving control of the library's information resources. They keep the library's collection of books and journals from being a useless pile of paper. Most libraries are arranged in a remarkably similar fashion and systems are generally consistent from library to library, regardless of size. Using libraries is somewhat like driving a standard transmission car. There are some differences from car to car but once a driver has mastered one, they are all mastered.

Library of Congress System

In nearly all academic libraries and most large public libraries, the Library of Congress (LC) classification scheme is used. This alphanumeric system groups the books into broad subject categories and then groups the broad subject categories into much smaller, more specific subject categories and finally, each of these specific subject categories is arranged alphabetically by author. The LC system serves two purposes at the same time, it arranges the books according to subject and serves as a location system for the library's resources.

The catalog is an index to the library's resources and has three components: author, title, and subject. The arrangement of the catalog will vary from library to library, but most libraries have either a dictionary or a divided catalog. A dictionary catalog is one in which all three components (author, title, and subject) are interfiled into a single continuous alphabetical arrangement. When the author and title components are filed alphabetically in one section and the subject component in another then the catalog is referred to as a divided catalog.

The subject section of the catalog in most libraries is based on the LIBRARY OF CONGRESS SUBJECT HEADINGS. This list of subject headings is a thesaurus of possibilities that can be used in building the subject component of the catalog. The use of a single thesaurus by all libraries lends great consistency to library catalogs and means that the mastery of this one tool represents the key to finding books in many libraries.

In addition to library catalogs many other bibliographic sources use LC subject headings to construct their subject access. BOOKS IN PRINT and all the H. W. Wilson indexes such as READER'S GUIDE and BUSINESS PERIODICALS INDEX are notable examples. A copy of LIBRARY OF CONGRESS SUBJECT HEADINGS is usually located near the public catalog as an aid for library users. It is important to check this before venturing into the catalog in order to identify the appropriate subject terms under which to search. The researcher who hasn't checked the LC subject list and doesn't find anything can't be sure whether the library has no books on that subject or whether the wrong subject heading was used.

The thesaurus of subject headings has many more "help" references than does the average catalog. The following symbols are used to designate the status of the various headings:

x: see reference

sa: see also reference

xx: see also from reference

The *x*, see reference, indicates that the term, although synonymous, is not used as a subject heading and refers the user to the correct term.

The *sa*, see also reference, means that the terms listed are related subjects which may contain information pertinent to the user's search. Catalogs and indexes often have see also references, usually at the beginning or end of the other subject entries.

The *xx*, see also from reference, is unique to subject headings lists. This reference establishes a chain by indicating a related heading from which a see also reference has been made. Literally, this can be described as a backwards see also reference. In other words, this term was used as a "see also" from the term in question.

Illustration 3.1
Example of a See Reference

Forebrain
  See Prosencephalon
Forecasting *(CB158)*
  sa Geophysical prediction
    Housing forecasting
    Prognosis
    Prophecy
    Social prediction
    subdivision Forecasts *under specific*
      centuries, e.g. Twentieth century—
      Forecasts
  x Futurology
    Prediction
  — Study and teaching *(Indirect)* *(CB158)*
    x Futures research
      Futures studies
Forecasting, Business
  See Business forecasting
Forecasting, Cloud
  See Cloud forecasting
Forecasting, Crime
  See Crime forecasting
Forecasting, Cyclone
  See Cyclone forecasting
Forecasting, Drought
  See Drought forecasting
Forecasting, Economic
  See Economic forecasting
Forecasting, Election
  See Election forecasting
Forecasting, Employment
  See Employment forecasting
Forecasting, Food consumption
  See Food consumption forecasting
Forecasting, Food supply
  See Food supply forecasting
Forecasting, Forest fire
  See Forest fire forecasting
Forecasting, Housing
  See Housing forecasting

Source: LIBRARY OF CONGRESS SUBJECT HEADINGS. 9th ed. Washington, D.C.: Library of Congress, 1980, page 892.

Illustration 3.2
Example of a See Also Reference

Future in literature   *(P.N56.F)*
● *sa* Eschatology in literature
      Science fiction
      Time in literature
   x Future as a theme in literature
   xx Science fiction
      Time in literature
Future interests   *(Indirect)*
● *sa* Executory interests
      Expectancies (Law)
      Perpetuities
      Remainders (Estates)
      Reversion
   x Future estates
   xx Estates (Law)
      Expectancies (Law)
      Property

Source: LIBRARY OF CONGRESS SUBJECT HEADINGS. 9th ed. Washington, D.C.: Library of Congress, 1980, page 929.

Library Filing Rules

With the advent of computer-generated catalogs some of the traditional filing rules are no longer observed. (See Appendix I for a list of library filing rules.) Online catalogs are filed according to the specific software designed especially for that library. Many times this software is based on traditional library practices which have been modified to take maximum advantage of the computer's power. Reference librarians are almost always on hand to assist library patrons in the use of the library's catalog whether it is in the form of cards or online.

Cataloging Records

When users are unable to locate the appropriate subject headings through the means described above there are at least two alternatives. The first is to request help from the reference librarian. This person has been hired specifically to help the researcher use the library's collection. No one should hesitate to request this person by title and to ask questions—the reference librarian's job is to answer questions. *The single most important reference tool is the reference librarian.*

The second alternative is to simply look up a book known to be relevant in the author/title section of the catalog. At the end of the cataloging record

Illustration 3.3
Example of a See Also From Reference

Pollution   *(Indirect)*   *(TD180)*
   sa Air—Pollution
     Electric power-plants—Environmental
       aspects
     Environmental engineering
     Factory and trade waste
     Marine pollution
     National Environmental Specimen
       Bank
     Noise pollution
     Pollution control industry
     Radioactive pollution
     Refuse and refuse disposal
     Soil pollution
     Spraying and dusting residues in
       agriculture
     Water—Pollution
     Water, Underground—Pollution
     subdivision Environmental aspects
       under individual environmental
       pollutants, e.g. Copper—
       Environmental aspects
   x Chemical pollution
     Chemicals—Environmental aspects
     Contamination of environment
     Environmental pollution
     Pollution—Control
     Pollution—Prevention
  xx Contamination (Technology)
     Environmental engineering
     Environmental health
     Environmental policy
     Factory and trade waste
     Man—Influence on nature
     Public health
     Refuse and refuse disposal
     Sanitary engineering
     Sanitation

Source: LIBRARY OF CONGRESS SUBJECT HEADINGS. 9th ed. Washington, D.C.: Library of Congress, 1980, page 1816.

Illustration 3.4
Example of Tracings

```
CB
158     World Future Society
W67         The Future: a guide to information
1979     sources.  Washington, D.C.:  World
        Future Society, 1979.

            viii, 722p., 25cm.

        Includes indexes.

            1. Forecasting - Societies, etc. -
        Directories.  2. Forecasting - Bibliog-
        raphy.            I. Title.
```

Illustration 3.5
Example of a Collation

```
CB
158     World Future Society
W67         The Future: a guide to information
1979     sources.  Washington, D.C.:  World
        Future Society, 1979.

            viii, 722p., 25cm.

        Includes indexes.

            1. Forecasting - Societies, etc. -
        Directories.  2. Forecasting - Bibliog-
        raphy.            I. Title.
```

there are several subjects and names listed and enumerated. When using an online catalog researchers will have to bring up the complete cataloging record in order to see the tracings as these names and subjects are called.

The Arabic numerals are subject tracings and the Roman numerals indicate joint authors, editors or alternative titles. The subject tracings mean that the book is entered in the catalog under all those subjects listed. By going to these subject headings other relevant materials can usually be located.

The collation or physical description of a book can also be useful to the researcher. This description includes the number of pages a book has as well as whether or not the book is illustrated. The collation for audiovisual materials lists the format and length as part of the physical description.

Illustration 3.6
Example of Notes

```
CB
158      World Future Society
W67          The Future: a guide to information
1979      sources.  Washington, D.C.:  World
         Future Society, 1979.

             viii, 722p., 25cm.

    ●    Includes indexes.

             1. Forecasting - Societies, etc. -
         Directories.  2. Forecasting - Bibliog-
         raphy.            ⌒   I, Title,
```

The notes are located immediately below the collation. This section can include such useful items as whether the work includes a bibliography or index or any other special features that the cataloger thinks are noteworthy.

A careful perusal of the catalog entry can save a great deal of time and effort that is frequently spent in locating a book that is not really suitable for the research in question.

Online Catalogs

Many libraries now have online catalogs in addition to, or instead of, the more traditional card catalogs. These online catalogs offer all the features of the conventional catalog on individual cards in addition to some more flexible search options. Since software for these catalogs varies from library to library few generalizations can be made concerning their use or their capabilities. Some online catalogs have the ability to search key words in the title that are not necessarily the first word in the title. Thus bibliographies can be compiled in this way as well as through the more traditional subject or author access. A typical online catalog entry provides even more information about a book than the traditional catalog card.

In addition to the usual bibliographic information such as the call number, author, and title, online catalogs usually tell whether or not a book is checked out.

Some libraries have their cards or online records printed in book form to replace the card catalog and still others have a microfiche catalog as a backup system for the online catalog. These alternative catalogs usually replace the card catalog entirely and supplement the online catalog and, of course, they are regularly updated. Many major libraries publish their card catalogs in book form and market them commercially. Thus, libraries may

Illustration 3.7
Example of Online Catalog Record

CALL NUMBER: WA/670/H434/1985   ACCN #: A165240

THE HEALTH DETECTIVE'S HANDBOOK; A GUIDE TO THE INVESTIGATION OF
ENVIRONMENTAL HEALTH HAZARDS BY NONPROFESSIONALS. EDITED BY MARVIN S.
LEGATOR, BARBARA L. HARPER, AND MICHAEL J. SCOTT. BALTIMORE, JOHNS
HOPKINS UNIVERSITY PRESS, C1985.
XV, 256P. ILLUS. 24CM.

      STATUS   DATE DUE   HOLDS
CHECKED OUT   04/07/87   0

OPTIONS: 1. TYPE B TO PAGE BACKWARD   2.
          3. TYPE C FOR CATALOG   4. TYPE I   TO RETURN TO INDEX
          5. ENTER NEW SEARCH HERE:
              THEN PRESS ENTER KEY :

have book catalogs from other libraries and these book catalogs can be very useful for doing in-depth research.

Interlibrary Loan Services and Referrals to Other Libraries

Many libraries have reciprocal borrowing privileges with other libraries and institutions regionally and nationally. Inquiries at the reference desk can provide researchers with information about local exchange policies and special borrower agreements, and about the means of locating a particular title in a nearby library. On a national level library networks can be used for interlibrary loan service which is generally offered at no charge to the borrowing library's card holders. This service usually includes the procuring of both books and journal articles. In essence, one library asks another library to loan them some materials on behalf of a patron and the lending library sends the material to the borrowing library which is responsible for its return.

Although interlibrary loans have entered the electronic age there are still some constraints that must be considered when this service is used. The major problem encountered is the time required. Materials are usually sent via U.S. mail, library rate, and one should allow at least two weeks for a request to be processed, filled, and mailed, although many requests will be filled in a shorter time. Another major obstacle, and one that adds greatly to the processing time, is an incomplete request by the patron. Any interlibrary loan request should include complete bibliographic information. In the case of a book this means: author, title, publisher, edition, date of publication, and the source of the preceding information.

In the case of a request for a journal article the necessary information includes: the journal title, volume, year of publication, author or authors of the article, title of the article, inclusive paging and the source of the preceding information.

A photocopy of the journal article will be sent by the lending library as most libraries will not loan the entire volume or issue of a journal. It is not necessary to return this photocopy to the lending library.

Most libraries have a specific form for requesting interlibrary loans and these should be used whenever possible to expedite the request.

Another problem encountered with an interlibrary loan request is that some parts of library collections may be used only within the confines of that particular library. Two common types of material that do not circulate are reference books and rare books. Reference books are usually compendiums of information in one format or another. THE ENCYCLOPÆDIA BRITANNICA and all the CRC handbooks are typical examples of works that might be in a reference collection. Chapter 4, General Reference Works, describes the kinds of books that usually fall into this category. Rare books are those considered valuable because of their age, unusualness, or scarcity.

Illustration 3.8
Example of an Interlibrary Loan Request for a Book

BOOK

INTERLIBRARY LOAN REQUEST FORM

REQUESTED BY _ALICE WYGANT_ DATE _3-22-87_

DEPT. AND EXT. NO. _Library, ext. 2398_

I DO NOT NEED THIS MATERIAL AFTER _May 1, 1987_

AUTHOR _Mary Scott Welch_

TITLE _NETWORKING_

EDITION _____

PUBLISHER _Warner Books_

YEAR OF PUBLICATION _1981_

SOURCE OF REFERENCE (OR VERIFIED IN) _Books in Print, 1986-87_

FOR LIBRARY USE ONLY:
LOCATION SOURCE AND LOCATION _____

_____

NOTES _____

☐ CCG   or   ☐ CCL

SENT _____

IL NO. _____

☐ OCLC   ☐ TWX   ☐ ALA

38

Illustration 3.9
Example of an Interlibrary Loan Request for a Journal Article

JOURNAL

INTERLIBRARY LOAN REQUEST FORM

REQUESTED BY _ALICE WYGANT_ DATE _3-22-87_

DEPT. AND EXT. NO. _LIBRARY, extension 2398_

I DO NOT NEED THIS MATERIAL AFTER _May 1, 1987_

JOURNAL TITLE, VOLUME, DATE _LIBRARY HI-TECH, vol. 3, 1985_

ARTICLE'S AUTHOR _Walt Crawford_

ARTICLE'S TITLE _Common sense and free software: or if it's free, can it be any good?_

INCLUSIVE PAGING _47-56_

SOURCE OF REFERENCE (OR VERIFIED IN) _Library Literature, Feb. 1986_

FOR LIBRARY USE ONLY:

LOCATION SOURCE _____

NOTES _____

☐ CCG   or   ☐ CCL

SENT _____

IL NO. _____

☐ OCLC   ☐ TWX   ☐ ALA

Any library has the right to declare any of its collection to be non-circulating. Policies vary from library to library and can present problems when certain types of material are requested.

Interlibrary loans are a service provided by libraries at great expense, and users have an obligation to conform to all the rules and policies imposed upon this service by the borrowing and the lending library. A careful examination of each request should be made before it is submitted and it should be evaluated using three questions as guidelines. Is the information complete? Is there time to use this service to secure materials? Is the material really necessary?

Special Libraries

When a researcher is involved in a project of a very specific nature, general academic and public libraries, however large and well equipped, may lack the specialized materials needed for this type of research project. In this case the researcher can usually identify special collections in the United States and Canada by using the DIRECTORY OF SPECIAL LIBRARIES AND INFORMATION CENTERS (9th ed., edited by Brigitte T. Darnay. Detroit: Gale Research Co., 1985). This directory serves as a guide to special libraries, research libraries, information centers, archives, and data centers of both a public and private nature. Over 16,000 libraries are listed alphabetically with more than 5,000 cross references to direct the user. There is also a subject index based on LIBRARY OF CONGRESS SUBJECT HEADINGS which includes numerous cross references. Extensive information is contained in each entry. Such information includes the name and address of the library and the institution it serves as well as the principal subjects represented in each library's collection.

Library Personnel

THE EXPERTISE OF LIBRARY PERSONNEL IS PERHAPS THE RESEARCHER'S MOST NEGLECTED RESOURCE! These people are specially trained to help researchers find the information needed in the fastest, most cost effective way. Almost all libraries, no matter how large or how small, have a reference department or at least a reference librarian. They are accustomed to dealing with research problems and can be a great help in locating the proper research tools or verifying references. They can also help the patron to take advantage of other library services such as interlibrary loans. *A word of caution*: not all people who work in libraries are librarians. Ask for the reference department or the reference librarian specifically; these people are professionally trained with at least one master's level degree. In addition to the basic requirement of a master's degree in library science many positions now require a second master's degree in a subject specialty. Researchers can only benefit by taking advantage of this training and expertise.

4

General Reference Works

General reference works are perhaps the most neglected source of information in the modern library. They represent a wealth of background materials and facts already assembled for the researcher. This is especially true for the person interested in future studies or planning issues. These researchers are often called upon to do papers or projects that deal with unfamiliar subject areas. There is no need to re-invent the wheel with each research endeavor. In most instances, basic background information has already been compiled; it's just a matter of locating the correct source. This chapter outlines some of the standard reference works and discusses the major types of reference books and their use for the futures researcher.

General Encyclopedias

Encyclopedias contain essays on a variety of topics. Generally, these essays are signed by subject specialists and scholars in the field and provide a summary of that topic as well as a short bibliography on the subject. They are useful in a number of ways. First, they provide readers with an introduction to a topic with which they may be unfamiliar. Second, they place the topic in a wider context and broaden the research base. And third, they serve as a starting point for further study. For the student, an encyclopedia article can provide the knowledge necessary to choose a topic for a research paper. By reading background information on a broad topic the student can choose a more specific aspect of the topic more intelligently.

When using an encyclopedia it is important to consult the index volume

44   Sources

Illustration 4.1
See Related References from Encyclopedia

Bibliography: Davies, J. Clarence, *The Politics of Pollution*, 2d ed. (1975); Hodges, Laurent, *Environmental Pollution*, 2d ed. (1977); Lund, Herbert F., *Industrial Pollution Control Handbook* (1971); Masters, Gilbert M., *Introduction to Environmental Science and Technology* (1974); Miller, G. Tyler, Jr., *Living in the Environment: Concepts, Problems, and Alternatives* (1975); Perkins, Henry C., *Air Pollution* (1974); Wagner, Richard H., *Environment and Man*, 2d ed. (1974).

●**See also:** CONSERVATION; ENVIRONMENTAL HEALTH; POLLUTANTS, CHEMICAL; WASTE DISPOSAL SYSTEMS.

Source: Article on "Pollution" in the ACADEMIC AMERICAN ENCYCLOPEDIA. Danbury, Conn.: Grolier, Inc., 1982, volume 15, page 416.

first. While the major listing for a subject may appear under the name of the subject alphabetically, there is almost certainly additional, relevant information under other subject entries. In addition, at the end of each article there are usually a number of see related references that refer to topics that may also be of interest to the reader.

Although no encyclopedia is updated every year, they all publish yearbooks. These annual publications serve as a synopsis of the year's events and highlight the developments in science and other fields. They are usually similar in format to the encyclopedia they accompany and should always be consulted in addition to the main body of the encyclopedia.

There are many fine general encyclopedias from which to choose. The two discussed below were selected as being representative of the genre.

ACADEMIC AMERICAN ENCYCLOPEDIA (Rev. ed., Danbury, Conn.: Grolier, Inc., 1986) is the first entirely new general encyclopedia to be published in more than a decade. Each edition is thoroughly reviewed and updated to reflect recent developments. As a comprehensive, general encyclopedia the ACADEMIC AMERICAN ENCYCLOPEDIA provides basic information in the summary essays and places that information in a historical or interpretive context. This work is especially valuable for its currency, its completeness, and its accuracy. In addition, it is extremely easy to use and is completely illustrated with a variety of photographs, charts, and drawings as well as the more traditional maps.

Its importance to researchers lies in its wealth of general information on any subject. In short, it can serve as a crash course on a particular country or political movement which, when completed, enables the researcher to move quickly on to more specific sources of information. The complete text of the ACADEMIC AMERICAN ENCYCLOPEDIA is now available online from DIALOG.

THE NEW ENCYCLOPÆDIA BRITANNICA's (15th ed., Chicago: Encyclopædia Britannica, Inc., 1974) 15th edition represents a departure from the traditional format of earlier editions. In the process of completely revising the 14th edition the editors divided the encyclopedia into three discrete sections. The Micropaedia, a series of ten volumes, serves a dual function as an index and as an educational resource. It contains short articles on topics and references to longer articles in the Macropaedia, a series of nineteen volumes. The Macropaedia contains longer articles that provide extended treatments of subjects. The Propaedia, a one-volume section, serves as an outline of knowledge and a guide to the encyclopedia as a whole. This three-part system is designed to meet the reader's information needs on a variety of levels.

The strengths of THE ENCYCLOPÆDIA BRITANNICA lie in its well deserved reputation and its ability to attract world renowned scholars as the authors of its subject essays and as members of its editorial board. Its new arrangement makes it more convenient to use in that the reader has the choice of a quick, "bare bones" approach in the Micropaedia or an exhaustive treatment of the subject in the Macropaedia.

Its chief importance to researchers lies in the Macropaedia. The information here is arranged in relation to other information so that a biographical article on Karl Marx is tied to a treatise on communism and its impact on world history. The Micropaedia has two paragraphs and a list of references on Marx while the Macropaedia has five pages on Marx and seven and a half pages on Marxism. The lack of knowledge of man's past experiences can be a great handicap to futurists and other researchers; and a quick perusal of the Macropaedia can be helpful in overcoming that handicap.

Handbooks

A handbook is a book of facts on a particular subject arranged especially for quick reference. Handbooks are used primarily for verification or to pinpoint an exact bit of information. For example, a researcher might need to find the population of the United States in 1960. In general, handbooks contain information that is static in nature, that is proven, and that is not subject to change under ordinary circumstances; population figures or mathematical values are typical examples. Handbooks are extremely useful as compendiums of data and, in most cases, there is a handbook for any subject or discipline. They do not contain original information but rather they draw together facts and data from many sources into one convenient place.

The CRC Press, Inc., of Cleveland, Ohio, publishes many handbooks which cover data in a wide range of scientific subjects.

The COMPOSITE INDEX FOR CRC HANDBOOKS (2d. ed., Cleveland, Ohio: CRC Press, 1977) covers all the CRC handbooks published even though each handbook has its own detailed index. This very useful tool provides access to all the handbooks at once through a subject index and a chemical substance index. This book is still useful even though many of

Illustration 4.2
Example from CRC Handbook

Table 4
SIGNS AND SYMPTOMS OF DEFICIENCIES AND EXCESSES OF MACROMINERALS

Elements	Deficiencies	Excesses
Calcium	Reduced growth, particularly of bone; osteoporosis and osetomalacia; hyperirritability and tetany; hemorrhage; parathyroid enlargement	Idiopathic hypercalcemia; milk alkali syndrome; hypercalcuria; renal calculus
Chloride	Alkalosis; deficiency of potassium; renal lesions; achlorhydria; hyperexcitability	
Magnesium	Irritability of CNS; susceptibility to atherosclerosis in some species; vasodilation	Depression of CNS; depression of cardiovascular system; reduces renal oxalate stone deposition
Phosphorus	decreased body growth; Decreased bone growth; rickets or osteomalacia; calcium citrate renal calculi; renal inanition	
Potassium	Adrenal hypertrophy; postpranidal hyperglycemia; reduced tissue glycogen; increased renal ammonia production; increased susceptibility to infection; growth reduction	Hypertrophy of zona glomerulosa; hyperkalemia
Sodium	Decreased growth	Hypertension; degenerative disease of arterioles and glomeruli
Sulfur	Reduced methionine, cysteine, thiamine and biotin synthesis	

From Hafez, E. S. E. and Dyer, I. A., *Animal Growth and Nutrition*, Lea & Febiger, Philadelphia, 1969, chap. 17. With permission.

Source: CRC HANDBOOK OF NUTRITIONAL SUPPLEMENTS, Volume II. Boca Raton, Fla.: CRC Press, 1983, page 55.

the handbooks it indexes have been updated. It can still be used to identify the appropriate handbook in which to look.

CRC publications serve as standards in this field. They have the highest reputation for accuracy and for comprehensive coverage of a field or subfield. For the researcher they provide a handle to sophisticated and complex information areas that would otherwise be denied the non-scientist.

THE COUNTY AND CITY DATA BOOK (10th ed., Washington, D.C.: Government Printing Office, 1983.) is one of the most notable handbooks published by the United States government. It contains statistical information derived from the U.S. census and covers all the standard metropolitan statistical areas (SMSA) as well as cities, urbanized areas, and unincorporated places. There is no index but there is a very detailed table of contents at the beginning of each volume which makes the information fairly accessible.

Illustration 4.3
Table from County and City Data Book

Table B. Counties — **Vital Statistics and Health Care**

County	Births, 1980 Number Total	Births, 1980 To mothers under 20 yrs. old (Per-cent)	Births, 1980 Rate[1]	Deaths, 1980 Number	Deaths, 1980 Rate[1]	Marriages, 1980 Number	Marriages, 1980 Rate[1]	Divorces, 1980 Number	Divorces, 1980 Rate[1]	Physicians, active non-Federal, 1980[2] (Yearend) Number	Physicians Rate[4]	Dentists, active, 1979[2] (Yearend)	Nurses, active, registered, 1977[2]	Hospitals, 1980[2] Num-ber	Hospitals, 1980[2] Beds Number	Hospitals Rate[4]
	30	31	32	33	34	35	36	37	38	39	40	41	42	43	44	4
LOUISIANA — Con.																
Catahoula	243	21.4	19.8	130	10.6	127	10.3	NA	NA	2	16.3	1	17	1	53	431.
Claiborne	302	28.1	17.7	187	10.9	118	6.9	NA	NA	8	46.8	4	31	2	88	514.
Concordia	452	29.4	19.7	225	9.8	222	9.7	85	3.7	8	34.8	6	20	1	50	217.
De Soto	480	28.5	18.7	310	12.0	204	7.9	103	4.0	5	19.4	3	19	1	55	213.
East Baton Rouge	7 039	15.2	19.2	2 381	6.5	3 922	10.7	1 923	5.3	606	165.5	164	1 179	7	1 934	528.
East Carroll	268	35.3	22.9	129	11.0	100	8.5	34	2.9	4	34.0	2	9	1	31	263.
East Feliciana	395	23.8	20.8	184	9.7	180	9.5	95	5.0	29	152.5	3	68	3	1 471	7 734.
Evangeline	635	23.6	19.0	333	10.0	381	11.4	135	4.0	21	63.0	3	55	2	223	668.
Franklin	449	30.7	18.6	252	10.4	260	10.4	120	5.0	8	37.5	3	24	1	55	227.
Grant	268	20.5	16.0	154	9.2	146	8.7	54	3.2	4	23.9	1	2	-	-	-
Iberia	1 460	20.7	22.9	524	8.2	751	11.8	303	4.8	62	97.3	23	92	3	223	349.
Iberville	685	24.2	21.3	321	10.0	307	9.5	109	3.4	20	62.2	8	58	3	461	1 433.
Jackson	308	28.6	17.6	200	11.5	164	9.5	NA	NA	8	46.2	3	24	1	67	386.
Jefferson	8 270	15.4	18.2	2 972	6.5	4 532	10.0	2 413	5.3	686	150.9	213	1 126	6	1 276	280.
Jefferson Davis	684	20.6	21.3	285	8.9	362	11.3	85	2.6	18	56.0	10	29	2	120	373.
Lafayette	3 098	16.0	20.7	884	5.9	1 718	11.5	435	2.9	247	164.6	86	468	5	792	527.
Lafourche	1 709	19.7	20.7	506	6.2	840	10.2	322	3.9	67	81.2	32	184	3	314	360.
La Salle	271	22.5	15.9	177	10.4	203	11.9	97	5.7	10	56.8	4	29	2	138	811.
Lincoln	551	19.6	13.9	301	7.6	312	7.8	NA	NA	34	85.5	10	89	1	126	321.
Livingston	1 188	18.3	20.2	361	6.1	604	11.8	299	5.1	9	15.3	15	23	1	52	86.
Madison	353	29.7	22.1	185	11.6	135	8.5	154	9.6	5	31.3	2	13	1	25	156.
Morehouse	723	30.3	20.8	342	9.6	277	8.0	126	3.6	20	57.5	5	46	1	110	316.
Natchitoches	696	21.6	17.5	431	10.8	341	8.6	136	3.4	23	57.7	7	57	1	119	298.
Orleans	10 353	20.7	18.6	6 258	11.2	5 075	9.1	2 780	5.0	2 315	415.2	346	3 045	19	6 354	1 123.
Ouachita	2 862	20.9	19.1	1 108	8.0	1 294	9.3	787	5.5	182	130.7	48	354	3	758	544.
Plaquemines	580	22.4	22.3	204	7.8	302	11.6	85	3.3	8	30.7	4	25	1	39	149.
Pointe Coupee	475	18.5	19.8	221	9.2	210	8.7	18	.7	9	37.4	3	25	1	29	120.
Rapides	2 499	21.9	18.5	1 232	9.1	1 592	11.8	759	5.6	190	140.4	50	619	8	3 703	2 737.
Red River	199	31.2	19.1	113	10.8	118	11.3	29	2.8	6	57.5	1	14	2	92	881.
Richland	446	23.8	20.1	257	11.6	201	9.1	128	5.8	15	67.6	6	29	2	116	531.
Sabine	381	27.3	15.1	231	9.1	227	9.0	79	3.1	10	39.6	4	34	3	139	549.
St. Bernard	1 103	17.8	17.2	506	7.9	974	15.2	347	5.4	15	23.4	15	53	2	148	230.
St. Charles	717	20.4	19.2	217	5.8	372	10.0	151	4.1	11	29.5	6	49	1	50	134.
St. Helena	153	24.8	15.6	65	6.6	105	10.7	43	4.4	2	20.4	-	11	1	35	356.
St. James	444	17.1	20.7	169	7.9	214	10.0	43	2.0	9	41.9	5	34	2	89	321.
St. John the Baptist	769	16.5	24.1	214	6.7	320	10.0	96	3.0	5	15.7	6	18	-	-	-
St. Landry	1 809	21.9	21.5	847	10.1	914	10.9	243	2.9	66	78.5	17	114	4	313	372.
St. Martin	913	18.8	22.7	307	7.6	351	8.7	113	2.8	8	19.9	5	18	2	51	126.
St. Mary	1 396	23.4	21.7	514	8.0	791	12.3	315	4.9	39	60.7	18	103	3	226	354.
St. Tammany	2 057	15.5	18.6	705	6.4	1 078	9.7	NA	NA	125	112.7	41	232	4	912	822.
Tangipahoa	1 706	22.3	21.1	726	9.0	662	10.7	139	1.7	44	54.5	22	147	4	326	404.
Tensas	166	27.1	19.5	111	13.0	61	7.2	28	3.3	4	46.9	1	15	1	30	351.
Terrebonne	2 422	19.0	25.7	596	6.3	1 266	13.4	602	6.4	79	83.7	33	187	1	186	197.
Union	354	24.9	16.7	232	11.0	139	6.6	71	3.4	10	47.2	2	25	2	60	283.
Vermilion	1 015	21.4	20.9	442	9.1	526	10.9	134	2.8	29	59.8	12	70	4	229	472.
Vernon	1 362	22.6	25.5	317	5.9	760	14.2	235	4.4	14	26.2	25	100	3	244	456.
Washington	825	23.6	18.7	473	10.7	491	11.1	83	1.4	35	79.2	13	123	3	258	583.
Webster	764	25.1	17.5	489	11.2	417	9.6	167	3.8	20	45.8	10	81	2	168	385.
West Baton Rouge	419	21.2	22.0	142	7.4	184	9.6	52	2.7	4	21.0	2	15	-	-	-
West Carroll	254	24.0	19.7	124	9.6	134	10.4	33	2.6	4	31.0	2	6	1	52	402.
West Feliciana	150	20.7	12.3	64	5.3	102	8.4	20	1.6	10	82.1	2	11	1	22	180.
Winn	303	24.8	17.6	251	14.5	171	9.9	72	4.2	8	46.4	5	20	1	96	568.
MAINE	16 461	15.3	14.6	10 766	9.6	12 040	10.7	46 205	45.5	1 623	144.3	489	6 263	52	6 848	608.
Androscoggin	1 512	16.7	15.2	932	9.4	1 012	10.2	620	6.2	158	158.5	42	602	3	537	538.
Aroostook	1 375	18.5	15.1	766	8.4	895	9.8	390	4.3	89	97.4	30	429	8	365	398.
Cumberland	3 039	12.8	14.1	2 114	8.8	2 375	11.0	1 175	5.4	509	235.9	143	1 824	5	1 492	691.
Franklin	374	17.9	13.8	207	7.6	291	10.7	135	5.0	30	110.7	10	82	1	186	397.
Hancock	615	13.3	14.7	454	10.9	539	12.9	237	5.7	57	136.4	24	194	4	1 582	1 439.
Kennebec	1 636	15.0	14.9	1 038	9.4	1 065	9.7	652	5.9	198	180.2	49	921	5	343	1 041.
Knox	469	13.9	14.2	387	11.7	411	12.5	208	6.3	65	197.3	17	175	2	88	264.
Lincoln	372	10.8	14.5	297	11.6	345	13.4	142	5.5	33	128.4	11	54	2	68	300.
Oxford	730	19.5	14.9	557	11.4	555	11.3	229	4.7	42	85.5	15	203	2	147	783.
Penobscot	1 956	16.8	14.3	1 113	8.1	1 344	9.8	904	6.6	212	154.7	56	773	7	1 074	783.
Piscataquis	271	14.0	15.4	210	11.9	205	11.6	101	5.7	15	85.1	5	71	3	110	623.
Sagadahoc	458	13.5	15.0	242	8.4	322	11.2	189	6.6	24	83.3	9	121	1	92	319.
Somerset	693	19.5	15.4	449	10.0	453	10.1	214	4.8	26	62.2	14	141	2	126	284.
Waldo	435	13.6	15.3	291	10.2	296	10.4	160	5.6	24	84.5	4	57	1	58	260.
Washington	536	22.9	15.3	443	12.7	378	10.8	181	5.2	22	62.9	11	138	2	115	328.
York	1 968	12.0	14.2	1 268	9.1	1 554	11.1	668	4.8	117	83.8	49	478	3	491	351.

[1]Per 1,000 resident population enumerated as of April 1.   [2]Data subject to copyright; see source citation.   [3]Excludes not classified.   [4]Per 100,000 resident population enumerated as April 1.   [5]Includes data not distributed by county.

Source: COUNTY AND CITY DATA BOOK. 10th ed. Washington, D.C.: Government Printing Office, 1983, page 244.

Yearbooks

Unlike handbooks, yearbooks emphasize the current year's information and they are published and updated more frequently because the inclusive information is constantly changing; for example, new officials are elected or appointed. The current issue of a yearbook is useful for the latest data available but the past issues are also useful for retrospective searching or for comparison with the data available currently.

There are almost as many yearbooks as there are subjects but a few of the most widely used and most representative are discussed below.

CONGRESSIONAL STAFF DIRECTORY (27th ed., edited by Charles B. Brownson and Anna L. Brownson. Mt. Vernon, Va.: Congressional Staff Directory, Ltd., 1985) contains useful information about Congress and the staffs of the members, committees, and subcommittees. There are over 3,000 staff biographies. Information about members of Congress and their staffs can prove invaluable to researchers who must be familiar with the workings and the people of the U.S. Congress.

THE STATESMAN'S YEARBOOK (123d ed., edited by John Paxton. New York: St. Martin's Press, 1986–87) is a standard reference source for information about international organizations and the countries of the world. It provides an excellent thumbnail sketch of the United Nations and its auxiliary agencies in addition to chapters covering other international organizations such as the Commonwealth and the Organizations of American States. In the latter part of the book each country of the world is dealt with individually in alphabetical order. Again, thumbnail sketches are provided that cover monetary systems, political organization, and principal industries.

Obviously the value of this yearbook lies in its ability to present the basic, necessary facts about a country or organization. To have this information handy in one continuously updated source is extremely important to futurists. The information is all secondary, that is, it is available in other scattered sources. The strength of THE STATESMAN'S YEARBOOK is that it brings all of this information together in one place.

YEARBOOK OF THE UNITED NATIONS 1982 (New York: United Nations, 1985) seeks to cover in capsule form the response of the United Nations to a wide variety of world problems. Since the problems facing the United Nations are those normally studied by futures researchers this yearbook is an excellent means of getting an overview of the world situation. Typical problems focused on include the status of women and the world's food supply as well as problems relating to specific geographical areas such as the Middle East.

THE WORLD ALMANAC AND BOOK OF FACTS (New York: Newspaper Enterprise Assn., Inc., 1987) is neither strictly a handbook or a yearbook. In fact, it has elements of both and some features unique to almanacs.

It has been published annually since 1886. There is a detailed, general index and a quick reference index to the data and facts covered. The general index is located in the *front* of the book along with the highlights of the year. This general reference work contains a wide variety of information on many topics ranging from the results of the latest census and elections in the United States to a capsule account of the year for the current U.S. president. In spite of its name, THE WORLD ALMANAC has a definite trend toward U.S. activities and data. In addition to current yearbook information it also contains much handbook information such as a table of weights and measures and their equivalents.

THE WORLD ALMANAC is indispensable for researchers because it contains such a wide spectrum of useful information. All of this information could be obtained from primary sources and so, again, the almanac's value lies in its compiling of all these sources into a single, inexpensive, secondary source.

Specialized Encyclopedias

Specialized encyclopedias serve the same purposes as general encyclopedias, they simply cover a much more specific subject area. There are encyclopedias on many subjects. The essays are usually written by recognized scholars and followed by a definitive bibliography on the subject covered. These essays can be extremely useful to the student or researcher in understanding and defining a topic and the bibliographies provide valuable suggestions for further reading.

The McGRAW-HILL ENCYCLOPEDIA OF SCIENCE AND TECHNOLOGY (5th ed., New York: McGraw-Hill Book Co., 1986) is an encyclopedia which provides comprehensive coverage of the physical, natural, and applied sciences. For each new edition every article from the previous edition is carefully evaluated and the facts, illustrations, and bibliographies are updated. Virtually any scientific topic except medicine is covered in the fifteen volumes of this reference tool and the index provides easy access to the information. An annual yearbook is published to keep the information current between editions.

Each article has an introductory paragraph or sentence that succinctly defines the topic. A more complex and detailed explanation usually follows the introductory definition. The McGRAW-HILL ENCYCLOPEDIA OF SCIENCE AND TECHNOLOGY is important to the researcher for its broad, general coverage of all aspects of science arranged in a convenient format. The articles use a jargon-free style that is easily understood by the non-scientist.

The INTERNATIONAL ENCYCLOPEDIA OF THE SOCIAL SCIENCES (edited by David L. Sills. New York: The Macmillan Co. and The Free Press, 1977) is one of the best known of the special encyclopedias. It is a seventeen volume work that includes articles on all aspects of anthropology, economics, geography, history, law, political sciences, psychiatry, psychology, sociology, and statistics. Because the articles are lengthy and many cover more than one subject it is especially important to consult the index volume. In addition, there are numerous cross references to guide the reader from essay to related essay. This encyclopedia is most useful for its broad, scholarly coverage of social sciences theory and its extensive bibliographies.

The ENCYCLOPEDIA OF PHILOSOPHY (edited by Paul Edwards. New York: The Macmillan Co. and The Free Press, 1973) is similar in format to the INTERNATIONAL ENCYCLOPEDIA OF THE SOCIAL SCIENCES. It is the major general reference book for philosophy and the only one to cover all aspects of this discipline and to deal with Eastern and Western philosophical thought as well as ancient, medieval and modern philosophers. It also discusses the work of mathematicians and other scientists whose theories have an impact on philosophy. All of the special encyclopedias published by Macmillan and The Free Press share the reputation for the highest caliber of scholarship and most comprehensive coverage. The ENCYCLOPEDIA OF PHILOSOPHY is extremely useful for beginning futurists because they can easily research those philosophers on whom future studies theories are based. Novices can also trace references to schools and trends of philosophical thought and place them in the context of philosophy as a whole.

Guides to the Literature

Guides to the literature identify sources of information available on a given subject. There are also a few guides that cover all subjects. One of the most notable of these is GUIDE TO REFERENCE BOOKS (10th ed., edited by Eugene Sheehy. Chicago: American Library Association, 1987). GUIDE TO REFERENCE BOOKS is frequently referred to as "Sheehy's" by librarians and other information specialists. It lists and evaluates reference sources in broad subject categories. Within each subject category titles are divided by type such as encyclopedias or dictionaries or indexes. Each entry is annotated and complete bibliographic information is given. Qualitative judgments are made concerning each entry as space is limited and only the best and most respected works from each subject are included. Sheehy's is the most comprehensive guide to resource materials of all kinds in existence today. Regular updates are published which keep it reasonably current. A look through Sheehy's can save a researcher untold amounts of time spent in random searching for source materials. It provides at a glance the major bibliographic resources for each subject area and describes their limitations and special features. Sheehy's has an excellent index by subject and title.

Another notable guide to the reference literature is the AMERICAN REF-ERENCE BOOKS ANNUAL (edited by Bohdan S. Wynar. Littleton, Colo.: Libraries Unlimited, Inc., 1970-   ). AMERICAN REFERENCE BOOKS ANNUAL serves as a comprehensive annual reviewing service for reference books published in the United States. This guide is most widely used by librarians as an aid in purchasing books. Since 1970 it has reviewed over 25,000 reference titles. These include not only recommended books; they represent all the reference works published in the preceding year. References to reviews published in the library literature during the year of coverage are appended to AMERICAN REFERENCE BOOKS ANNUAL reviews. Types of reference books covered are: bibliography, periodicals and serials, publishing and bookselling, encyclopedias, directories, handbooks and year-books, abbreviations, almanacs, government publications, proverbs, quo-tation books, style manuals, and biography.

AMERICAN REFERENCE BOOKS ANNUAL and GUIDE TO REF-ERENCE BOOKS are valuable tools for the researcher as they identify and annotate all the major reference books available. The former is more com-prehensive for American reference books and is updated more often but the latter has a more convenient format for the novice and is more selective in its coverage.

KEYS TO LIBRARY RESEARCH ON THE GRADUATE LEVEL: A GUIDE TO THE GUIDES by Harvey R. Gover (Washington, D.C.: Uni-versity Press of America, 1981) is a short almost pamphlet-like book that is a down-to-earth guide to using the library. Mr. Gover covers all the major facts of using the library and lists books which elaborate on his information. There are numerous examples, both illustrative and anecdotal, to describe the various guides and library procedures.

MATERIALS AND METHODS FOR SOCIOLOGICAL RESEARCH by James Gruber and Judith Pryor (New York: Neal-Schuman Pub., Inc., 1980) is another excellent guide to library research in general and sociological research in particular. The authors have compiled a guide and a workbook designed to teach the beginning sociologist what is available in most libraries and how to find it. Unlike Gover's guide this one includes exercises with each chapter that reiterate the points made in the text of the chapter through practical applications. This work also examines the use of scholarly journals in research and how to evaluate a book length study. It is especially useful to futurists and futures students since sociological literature forms the back-bone of futures research materials, and many bibliographic tools and data resources are common to both fields.

Another extremely useful book, THE REPORTER'S HANDBOOK: AN INVESTIGATOR'S GUIDE TO DOCUMENTS AND TECHNIQUES by Investigative Reporters and Editors under the editorship of John Ullmann and Steve Honeyman (New York: St. Martin's Press, 1983) is designed to teach investigative reporters how to follow paper trails and thus find key documents with which they can bolster their stories. The book is based on the premise that such reporters need to find out how the system is supposed to work. The detailed table of contents lists such chapters and sub-chapters as "The Freedom of Information Act" and "Getting a Hold of Recently Declassified Materials" as well as "Investigating Politicians." THE RE-PORTER'S HANDBOOK provides immediate access to documentation of all kinds in a step-by-step, readable format.

Reference Books for Futurists

FUTURES SURVEY (edited by Michael Marien. Washington, D.C.: World Future Society, 1979-   ), FUTURE SURVEY ANNUAL (edited by Michael Marien. Washington, D.C.: World Future Society, 1979-   ), and SOCIETAL DIRECTIONS AND ALTERNATIVES by Michael Marien (Lafayette, N.Y.: Information for Policy Design, 1976) are all guides to the available futures literature. FUTURES SURVEY is "a monthly abstract of books, articles, and reports concerning forecasts, trends, and ideas about the future." These monthly issues are cumulated annually in FUTURE SUR-VEY ANNUAL. Aside from their obvious use as current awareness tools these surveys serve as a guide to what has been published as well as what is currently being published. They are indexed by author and subject and bring together all of the materials published on future studies into one convenient source.

SOCIETAL DIRECTIONS AND ALTERNATIVES discusses problems in the context of their bibliographic references. This book is of special value to novice futurists because the major futures works are placed with other works that deal with that problem or concept. In addition to the problem-oriented sections there are chapters on background information, antholo-gies, and symposia and miscellaneous works. The book's usefulness is greatly increased by its nine indexes which index by author, organization, chron-ological book title, evolutionary stage theories, titles of alternative societies, selected proposals, selected criticism, subject, and ideas.

There are several books that do not fit comfortably in any category but are nonetheless vital bibliographic resources for futurists. Two of these are guides not only to the literature but to the field in general. THE FUTURE: A GUIDE TO INFORMATION SOURCES (2d ed., edited by Edward Cor-nish. Washington, D.C.: World Future Society, 1979) is a special guide which covers organizations, individuals, and research projects as well as various types of nonprint media. It is basically a reference book for ongoing futures projects and practicing futurists and as such is an essential source for networking information. The geographical and subject indexes enhance an already useful book. The "individuals" section of this book has been updated as THE FUTURES RESEARCH DIRECTORY: INDIVIDUALS

(Washington, D.C.: World Future Society, 1986) which is discussed in Chapter 11, Other Media, Experts, Computer Software and Unpublished Sources.

THE FUTURE FILE: A GUIDE FOR PEOPLE WITH ONE FOOT IN THE 21ST CENTURY by Paul Dickson (New York: Avon Books, 1977) is written on a smaller scale, but is very similar in scope to THE FUTURE. It attempts to describe the futures resources available in the context of the field as a whole. Dickson's book is an essay on the future that is literally packed with information. Although it lacks the organization of some other works, THE FUTURE FILE is readable and serves as an excellent introduction to futures research and its tools.

THE BOOK OF KEY FACTS by The Queensbury Group (New York: Ballantine Books, 1978) provides history at a glance and in concise form, both of which are necessary in futures research, as futurists frequently study the past in order to apply it to the future. THE BOOK OF KEY FACTS is a guide to what, when and where it happened. It is arranged by year and begins with 30,000 B.C. and ends with 1978. It has an excellent index and many useful appendixes.

Conclusion

The general reference works discussed in this chapter are merely a scant few of the dozens of useful reference works available to the researcher. More specific subjects will require different reference books. As in all library research, the reference librarian can be of great help to the researcher and should be consulted early in the research project for suggestions. PROFESSIONAL REFERENCE LIBRARIANS ARE UNDOUBTEDLY THE SINGLE MOST USEFUL REFERENCE TOOL AVAILABLE TO THE RESEARCHER.

5

Abstracts and Indexes

Indexes and abstracts provide the researcher with a means of accessing the information published in journals and most other serial publications such as conference proceedings. They are analogous to the catalog in a library. Just as the catalog guides the researcher to a particular book or books so the abstract or index identifies for the researcher an article or group of articles on a specific subject or by a specific author. The use of these tools is an essential skill for any researcher. There are thousands of journals currently being published and without abstracting and indexing services the information they contain would be almost inaccessible. It is not enough for researchers to be familiar with only a couple of indexing and abstracting services; they must be able to identify the appropriate service in a field of hundreds and know how to use it effectively if they are to do cross-disciplinary research.

Abstracting and indexing services delineate a group of journals and then index them by at least author and subject and often by a variety of other access points, such as report number, as well. The delineation usually follows the lines of a subject or an academic discipline. Indexes provide complete bibliographical citations which generally include: the journal issue, date, and the inclusive paging of the article in addition to the author(s) and the title of the article. Abstracts include the same sort of bibliographic information and in addition, they have a brief summary of the article.

Due to the added burden of writing a summary for each article indexed, abstracting services are generally working with materials published several months previously. Indexes are a little more current but they too lag behind the latest published material. The time lag problem is solved in part by online databases. Publishers of indexing and abstracting services make the magnetic tapes from which their services are printed available online. These databases are always more current than the printed copy and are updated more frequently. (See Chapter 6, Online Resources, for more information about databases.)

Subject access for indexes and abstracts is either based on a thesaurus of subject terms peculiar to the tool or a standardized list such as LIBRARY OF CONGRESS SUBJECT HEADINGS, or on some form of free text system in which significant words from the article's title and abstract are used to index the article. Each method has its advantages and the researcher needs to be aware of the pros and cons of both systems.

Thesaurus-based indexes use a controlled vocabulary of terms to classify articles and to integrate them into the system. The major advantage to this practice lies in the fact that the indexer examines the article, chooses a number of subject terms that best describe it, and enters the article's bibliographic information under each of those subject terms. Because a common term is chosen to cover all the synonyms for a concept the researcher needs to look under only one term per concept.

This controlled vocabulary format is a very complex system of interrelated terms and changes in the system may lag behind the field nomenclature. A concept may be part of the researcher's vocabulary for several years before it becomes part of the thesaurus.

On the other hand, with free text subject indexes this is not the case. As soon as an author uses a word in the title of an article that word becomes part of the subject indexing system in a free text index. This indexing is generally done using a computer which is programmed to delete words such as "a," "an," "and," "the," or prepositions as well as certain stop words. The computer then alphabetizes those words that remain. Although this system means that the index can be generated more quickly and that the author's language immediately becomes part of the index, it also means that the researcher must look under the singular and plural forms of the term in question as well as all the synonyms for that term. The computer usually defines a word as a group of characters bounded by punctuation or a space; consequently different forms of the same word and synonyms of that word are all perceived as entirely different and unrelated words by the computer and are indexed accordingly.

Obviously both types of indexing are necessary to researchers. If the concept being investigated is a relatively new one then a key word, free text index is the better choice. On the other hand, if the concept has many synonyms then a thesaurus approach is preferred. As a general rule there are several indexes or abstracts for each subject area so researchers can choose the style that best fits their search parameters.

ULRICH'S INTERNATIONAL PERIODICALS DIRECTORY (25th ed.

Illustration 5.1
Example of Thesaurus Entry

FUTURES (OF SOCIETY)   *Jun. 1973*
    CIJE: 4425   RIE: 3330   GC: 520
UF   Alternative Futures
     Educational Futures #
     Future Studies
     Futurism
     Futuristics
     Futurology
RT   Appropriate Technology
     Culture Lag
     Decision Making
     Delphi Technique
     Emerging Occupations
     Long Range Planning
     Planning
     Prediction
     Public Policy
     Relevance (Education)
     Revolution
     Science And Society
     Social Change
     Social Indicators
     Technological Advancement
     Trend Analysis
     Values
     World Affairs

Futures Planning
USE LONG RANGE PLANNING

Futurism
USE FUTURES (OF SOCIETY)

Futuristics
USE FUTURES (OF SOCIETY)

Futurology
USE FUTURES (OF SOCIETY)

Source: THESAURUS OF ERIC DESCRIPTORS. 11th ed. Phoenix, Ariz.; Oryx Press, 1987, page 98.

New York: Bowker, 1986.) is a comprehensive list of all the periodicals, both foreign and domestic, which are currently being published. It is extensively updated every two years and has quarterly supplements to the biannual two-volume directory. Periodical titles are listed by subject and are indexed by title at the end of the second volume. Fairly extensive information is given for each title listed. This information includes: journal title, subtitle, publisher, place of publication, information on journal con-

Illustration 5.2
Example of Free Text Subject Index

NESTED
A COMPARATIVE ANALYSIS BETWEEN THE FINANCIAL
INSTABILITY HYPOTHESIS AND THE MONETARY
THEORY OF DEEP DEPRESSIONS FOR THE INTERWAR
PERIOD A NON-NESTED TEST OF HYPOTHESIS
(BUSINESS CYCLES, ECONOMIC FLUCTUATIONS, DEBT
DEFLATION) (ECONOMICS, THEORY) GOMEZ, RICHARD
JAMES, p.2266-A

NETHERLANDS
PAMPHLETS, PRINTING, AND POLITICS IN THE EARLY
DUTCH REPUBLIC (NETHERLANDS) (HISTORY,
EUROPEAN) HARLINE, CRAIG EDWARD, p.2284-A

NETWORK
A STOCHASTIC GENERALIZED NETWORK MODEL AND
LARGE-SCALE ALGORITHM FOR PORTFOLIO
SELECTION AND TIMING IN THE FREQUENCY DOMAIN
AND AN EMPIRICAL EVALUATION OF PORTFOLIO
PERFORMANCE (MANAGEMENT, FINANCE,
INVESTMENTS) (BUSINESS ADMINISTRATION,
GENERAL) JONES, C. KENNETH, p.2220-A
A STRUCTURAL ANALYSIS OF REFERENCES TO HEALTH
ON AMERICAN PRIME TIME NETWORK TELEVISION
(CULTURAL ANTHROPOLOGY, NURSING) (EDUCATION,
HEALTH) FOX, JANE ANN, p.2034-A
EXPERIENCING PERSONAL NETWORK COMMUNITIES
(SOCIOLOGY, GENERAL) LEIGHTON, BARRY NOEL,
p.2324-A
THE COMMUNICATION NETWORK AS INTERPRETIVE
ENVIRONMENT "SENSE-MAKING" AMONG
BIOMEDICAL RESEARCH SCIENTISTS (MASS
COMMUNICATIONS) LIEVROUW, LEAH ANNE,
p.1914-A
THE DECENTRALIZATION OF AN AMBULATORY HEALTH
CARE SERVICES NETWORK SPATIAL ACCESSIBILITY
OF PRENATAL CARE SERVICES IN SELECTED AREAS OF
BOSTON (MASSACHUSETTS) (URBAN AND REGIONAL
PLANNING) FREEMAN, A. MARK, p.2341-A

NETWORKING
EDUCATIONAL REFORM AN EXPLORATORY ANALYSIS
OF MAJOR NEWSPAPERS' COVERAGE OF "A NATION
AT RISK" (STATUS CONFERRAL NETWORKING, AGENDA
SETTING, CONTENT ANALYSIS, GATEKEEPING)
(EDUCATION, GENERAL) ZABRANSKEY, MARGARET
LUCILLE, p.1933-A
INTERAGENCY NETWORKING IN ENERGY-IMPACTED
RURAL AREAS THE SOCIAL SERVICE PERSPECTIVE
(ORGANIZATIONAL RELATIONSHIPS, ENERGY
DEVELOPMENT) (SOCIAL WORK) DELEWSKI,
CATHERINE HANES, p.2317-A

NETWORKS
"MY FAMILY IS ME" WOMEN S KIN NETWORKS AND
SOCIAL POWER IN A BLACK SEA ISLAND COMMUNITY
(SOUTH CAROLINA) (ANTHROPOLOGY, CULTURAL)
DAY, VIRGINIA KAY YOUNG p.2213-A
AGING IN A NATIVE AMERICAN COMMUNITY SERVICE
NEEDS AND SUPPORT NETWORKS AMONG PRAIRIE
BAND POTAWATOMI ELDERS (INDIANS, FRIENDSHIP,
FAMILY, SIBLINGS, CHILDREN KANSAS) (SOCIOLOGY,
INDIVIDUAL AND FAMILY STUDIES) JOHN, ROBERT,
p.2332-A
AN APPROACH TO PLANNING FOR PROFESSIONS WITH
APPLICATION TO THE PROFESSION OF PHARMACY
(NETWORKS, EPIDEMIOLOGY SOCIOTECHNICAL
SYSTEMS) (BUSINESS ADMINISTRATION, GENERAL)
LAWRENCE, ARTHUR JOHN JR, p.2221-A
A SENSE OF PLACE URBAN INDIANS AND THE HISTORY
OF PAN-TRIBAL INSTITUTIONS IN PHOENIX, ARIZONA
(NETOWRKS, ETHNICITY ANTHROPOLOGY,
CULTURAL) LIEBOW, EDWARD B , p.2215-A

Source: DISSERTATIONS ABSTRACTS INTERNATIONAL. Ann Arbor, Mich.: University
Microfilms International, 1986, volume 47A(6), page 137.

Illustration 5.3
Example from Ulrich's

500   **US   ISSN 0016-3317**
FUTURIST; a journal of forecasts, trends, and ideas about
the future. 1967. bi-m. $25. World Future Society, 4916
St. Elmo Ave., Bethesda, MD 20814. TEL 301-656-8274
Ed. Timothy H. Willard. adv. bk. rev. charts. illus.
cum.index: 1967-1975, 1976-1980, 1981-1982. circ. 30,
000. (also avail. in microform from UMI; back issues
avail.; reprint service avail from UMI) Indexed:
Curr.Cont. R.G. SSCI. Sci.Abstr. Soc.Sci.Ind.
Bk.Rev.Ind. BPIA. Bus.Ind. Abstrax. C.I.J.E.
Comput.Bus. Educ.Admin.Abstr. Fut.Surv. Lang.&
Lang.Behav.Abstr. Manage.Cont. Mag.Ind. PMR.
PROMT. Pers.Lit.

Source: ULRICH'S INTERNATIONAL PERIODICAL DIRECTORY, 1986–87. New York:
R. R. Bowker, 1986, page 1511.

tent, and where the periodical is indexed. All but the last two are self-
explanatory bits of information. The facts provided about the journal content refer to whether or not it has reviews of any kind, the type of illustrations
it has, and whether or not it has advertisements. What is perhaps the most
important information is given last: *where the journal is indexed.* Using
abbreviations ULRICH'S indicates which of the abstracting and indexing
services index each periodical title.

ULRICH'S is extremely useful for identifying the appropriate abstract or
index to use. The researcher simply checks a number of journal titles that
are appropriate to his research project and determines the indexing and
abstracting tools that are represented in most of the ULRICH'S entries for
these journals.

There are literally hundreds of indexing and abstracting services dealing
with periodicals from every conceivable field. It would be impossible to
cover all of them in the scope of this book. The ones discussed below are
representative of the tools available in both format and contents and are
generally available in most libraries.

BUSINESS PERIODICALS INDEX (BPI) (New York: H. W. Wilson Co.,
1958-   ) is a subject index to approximately 170 periodicals in the fields
of accounting, advertising, banking and finance, general business, insurance,
labor and management, marketing and purchasing, public administration,
taxation, industries and trades. It is issued monthly and cumulated annually.

BPI is published by the H. W. Wilson Company which also publishes
READER'S GUIDE TO PERIODICAL LITERATURE as well as a number
of other indexes on a wide variety of subjects. (See Appendix II for a
complete list of Wilson indexes.) These tools all use LIBRARY OF CON-
GRESS SUBJECT HEADINGS as their controlled vocabulary and thus, once

the appropriate subject headings are identified they can be used both in the library's catalog and any of the "Wilson" indexes.

These indexes provide quick access to a broad range of materials in an easy to use format. Specialized indexes such as these are useful because the subject terms are usually more specific and the researcher does not have to deal with as large a body of information as in the more specialized indexes. They are also readily available in almost any library.

"Wilson" indexes are also available online through WILSONLINE which is discussed in more detail in Chapter 6, Online Resources.

SOCIOLOGICAL ABSTRACTS (SA) (New York: Sociological Abstracts, 1952-   ) indexes a large number of journal titles in the field of sociology as well as other types of documents such as conference proceedings and dissertations. The documents are indexed by author and subject and arranged according to a standardized format which groups the articles by broad subject areas such as "mass phenomena" or "social differentiation" or "political interactions." These subject areas can be used as a current awareness tool as well as a bibliographic source of information. For instance, researchers who are interested in the "sociology of leisure" need only to consult the table of contents of SA each month to see the latest articles published in that area. SA provides three points of access to each article: the table of contents, the subject index, and the author index. Its index format is similar to most other abstracting services: the index does not provide bibliographic information but rather all three points of access refer to accession numbers by which the complete bibliographic information and the abstracts are arranged chronologically.

PUBLIC AFFAIRS INFORMATION SERVICE (PAIS) (New York: Public Affairs Information Service, Inc., 1915-   ) has a selection policy which is slightly different from most other indexing and abstracting services. Instead of choosing a subject and identifying and indexing a list of journals which cover that subject, PAIS aims to identify the public affairs information most likely to be useful and interesting to legislators, administrators, businessmen, policy researchers, and social science students and professionals. Their multi-disciplinary concept approach includes everything from economics to education. Approximately 400 journals are scanned regularly for articles within the scope of PAIS.

Books are also indexed and priority is given to books that are systematic investigations of specific policy issues. A special effort is made to include all the available statistical sources regarding trade between countries. Publications of national, state, and intergovernmental organizations are selectively indexed according to their relevance to PAIS selection policies. Documents from foreign countries and intergovernmental agencies are not indexed in any other U.S. service and their inclusion in PAIS greatly enhances its value.

PAIS is indexed by author and subject. The latter is based on a controlled, standardized thesaurus and each entry appears under a minimum of one to a maximum of four subject headings. PAIS is issued weekly and cumulated five times a year with an annual bound volume serving as the final cumulation for each year.

Although the indexes and abstracts mentioned above are representative of the field, they constitute a very small number of the indexing and abstracting services available. An investigation of several libraries will yield a broad range of useful sources. Reference librarians are skilled users of such services and will be happy to help researchers learn to use them. In addition, each service includes detailed instructions for use in every volume and many libraries provide classes and/or materials about using indexes and abstracts.

FACTS ON FILE (FOF) (New York: Facts on File, 1940-   ) contains information about current events and is a looseleaf digest of world news that is updated weekly and cumulated annually with a bound volume. The stories are indexed in depth and the salient facts are presented in a few paragraphs. Sometimes researchers find this information sufficient and if not, they have enough information to go to the newspaper files and read more detailed accounts of the event in question. FOF can provide access to local newspapers whose indexes are not always readily accessible to the general public.

THE NEW YORK TIMES INDEX (NYTI) (New York: New York Times, 1913-   ) began indexing this major national newspaper in 1913. Its subject index gives an exact reference to date, page, and column of the article. An abundance of cross references helps the reader to identify his subject and pinpoint the reference. Entries also include brief synopses of the articles indexed making it possible in many cases to find the information needed without consulting the newspaper itself. The NYTI is issued semimonthly and cumulated annually. Many libraries have both the NYTI and THE NEW YORK TIMES. The former is often found in print while the latter is in microform. In addition to providing access to one of the United States' major social and political forums, the NYTI can serve as an index to other more regional newspapers in the same way FACTS ON FILE does.

Citation Indexes

The citation indexes are one of several products and services distributed through the Institute for Scientific Information (ISI). ISI was founded in the early 1960s by Eugene Garfield. Dr. Garfield's innovative approach to indexing and information retrieval has made ISI into one of the major vendors of bibliographic services in today's information market.

The unique features of ISI's publications are their depth of indexing, their indexing of the monograph literature and proceedings literature, and their indexing of citations in bibliographies and footnotes. Most indexing and abstracting services selectively index at least some of the journals they cover and the so-called peripheral material such as book reviews is rarely covered at all. ISI publications cover everything in a core collection of the journals they index and in some cases, such as SCIENCE CITATION INDEX, all the journals are fully covered. Only the advertisements are not indexed. This means that book reviews, obituaries, meeting notices and abstracts, letters, and even errata are indexed in ISI publications. They also cover a portion of the monograph literature not otherwise indexed and an entire index is devoted to conference proceedings. These last two groups of materials are rarely covered by other indexes and abstracts and yet are extremely valuable sources of information.

Finally and most importantly, not only do ISI publications index everything except the advertisements in selected lists of journals but they also index all of the citations and footnotes as well as the articles themselves. This citation indexing makes them unique and increases their value a hundred fold. The rationale behind citation indexing is that researchers find many of their key papers by examining the bibliography of a relevant paper and then going to those articles and their bibliographies and so on. The use of this "snowball" or "fan" approach led to the creation of citation indexes.

Both SOCIAL SCIENCES CITATION INDEX, SCIENCE CITATION INDEX, and ARTS AND HUMANITIES CITATION INDEX are arranged in a similar format with three major indexes: citation, source, and permuterm; and one minor index: corporate.

The citation index is composed of all the citations in all of the bibliographies and footnotes of the articles indexed. The citations are organized alphabetically by author. Each citation is followed by a list of those articles that cited it, which are also arranged alphabetically by author. This procedure is carried through for each indexing period. A cited item can be a book, journal article, letter, thesis or any other published or unpublished document. The only criterion for inclusion is that they are cited in the materials covered during that indexing period. Cited references are not bounded by time: if Aristotle is cited in an article in 1987, then Aristotle will appear in the citation index for 1987 and the reference citing him will be listed below his citation. Complete bibliographic information is not given in the citation index but enough information is given to identify the reference and locate it if necessary.

The citing reference will also appear in the source index or author index which is simply an alphabetical list of all the authors who published in the journals covered during the indexing period. It provides complete bibliographic information along with the first author's affiliation and address and the number of references in the article. Each source entry that is not an article has an identifier which indicates the nature of the selection, i.e., "M" stands for meeting notice or meeting abstract. The permuterm index discussed below refers the user to the source index.

The articles and other materials indexed by author in the source index

Illustration 5.4
Example from Citation Index

Citation Index — To locate recent articles in which older, known critical works are cited.

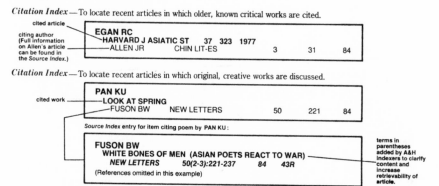

Citation Index — To locate recent articles in which original, creative works are discussed.

Source: Reprinted with permission from the *Arts & Humanities Citation Index* 1985 annual. Copyright 1986 by the Institute for Scientific Information, Pa.

Illustration 5.5
Example from Source Index

Source Index — To find current articles by known authors and to locate full bibliographic information.

journal					article title
	EGAN RC				
	POEMS ON PAINTINGS—SU, SHIH AND HUANG, TING-CHIEN				
	~HARV J ASIA	43(2):413-451	84	111R	number of references
author address	—HARVARD UNIV. CAMBRIDGE. MA 02138, USA				
	BUSH S	71	CHINESE LITERATI PAI		
	CHIU CA		TU FU CHINAS GREATES		
	HUANG TC		TI WEI YEN MA		
	"		TZUYUN HSIEN HUANG T		references
	PAN KU		HAN SHU		(only a partial list
	SU SHIH		SUNG FUKU HUA HSIAOH		of the references
	"		SHU WANG TINGKOU SOT		is shown here.)
	TU FU		KO CHIN		
			WEI FENG LUSHIH CHAI		
	YOSHIKAWA K	67	INTRO SUNG POETRY		

Source: Reprinted with permission from the *Arts & Humanities Citation Index* 1985 annual. Copyright 1986 by the Institute for Scientific Information, Pa.

are indexed by subject in the permuterm index. This section is a key word, free text index with a special twist: each word from the article title is paired with every other word from that title.

This method of permuting words from selection titles ensures that their relationship to each other is emphasized while making the procedure compatible with machine indexing.

The last index takes the authors listed alphabetically in the source index and rearranges them by institution in the corporate index. This index is first arranged alphabetically by country, then alphabetically by city within each country, and finally by institution within each city. Authors are arranged alphabetically under each institution. Thus, if you are interested in the authors publishing under the auspices of a particular institution, such as Stanford Research Institute, the corporate index can provide that list of authors.

Illustration 5.6
Example from Permuterm Index

Subject Index—To find current articles which have words, names and phrases relevant to the search topic in their titles.

Source Index entry for item by WANG ZL with words 'China' and 'poetry' in title:

Source: Reprinted with permission from the *Arts & Humanities Citation Index* 1985 annual. Copyright 1986 by the Institute for Scientific Information, Pa.

Illustration 5.7
Example from Corporate Index

Corporate Index—To find articles of interest when a corporate or academic institution is known to publish work on a topic.

MASSACHUSETTS CAMBRIDGE • HARVARD UNIV				
EGAN RC	HARV J ASIA	43	413	84
OWEN S	HARV J ASIA	43	711	84

Source: Reprinted with permission from the *Arts & Humanities Citation Index* 1985 annual. Copyright 1986 by the Institute for Scientific Information, Pa.

Each year ISI publishes a detailed guide for each of its publications. The guide describes the use of the various indexes in great detail and explains how to execute various types of searches in ISI publications. In addition, it lists the journals indexed by abbreviation, by full title, by country, and by subject. Books indexed are assigned an accession number which is then used to indicate that book in the other indexes. The guide always contains a list of indexed books by accession number.

Although ISI publications are slightly more difficult to use than some other sources they are the most powerful of the print tools available to researchers. They enable the user to track information both backward and forward in time. They make it easy to trace the use of a key technique or a definitive article, and they allow the researcher to use current field nomenclature to search the literature. Since they cover broad areas like the sciences or social sciences they are also especially useful for those who do multi-disciplinary research.

SOCIAL SCIENCES CITATION INDEX (SSCI) (Philadelphia: Institute for Scientific Information, 1966-   ) provides the most comprehensive coverage of the social sciences available. Over 4,300 journals are indexed; of these, 1,500 are full covered and the remainder are selectively indexed. The 4,300 journals represent the fields of anthropology, archaeology, business, communication, community health, criminology, demography, economics, education, ethics, ethnic studies, geography, history, information science, international relations, law, linguistics, management, marketing, philosophy, political science, psychiatry, psychology, sociology, statistics, and urban planning. In addition to journals SSCI also indexes non-journal materials such as monographic series, proceedings, and symposia.

The format of SSCI follows the traditional ISI structure of citation, source, and permuterm indexes. These three separate but related indexes provide the researcher with a tool that enables him to search across disciplines and to avoid the time lag to some extent and, at the same time, to keep abreast of current information being published. The language of the social sciences is frequently undergoing changes and the Permuterm Subject Index uses the exact language of the field scientist's title in its indexing.

SSCI is available online through both BRS and DIALOG.

SCIENCE CITATION INDEX (SCI) (Philadelphia: Institute for Scientific Information. 1961-   ) indexes over 3,000 scientific journals using the ISI format described above. Like SSCI, SCI is multi-disciplinary and the following general areas of science are represented: agriculture, biology, environmental studies, engineering, technology, medicine, physics, chemistry, and behavioral sciences. All of the 3,000 plus journals are indexed from cover to cover except for the advertisements. This phenomenal indexing task has resulted in the coverage of over seven million items since the index began in 1961.

SCI is available online through DIALOG only.

ARTS AND HUMANITIES CITATION INDEX (AHCI) (Philadelphia: Institute for Scientific Information, 1976-   ) is an index to worldwide literature of the arts and humanities. This multi-disciplinary index covers archaeology, architecture, art, classics, dance, film, folklore, history, language and linguistics, literature, music, philosophy, theater, theology and religion, television, and radio. In addition to every substantive item from more than 1,300 journals in the arts and humanities, AHCI also includes several thousand items a year that are selected from other ISI databases. AHCI is similar in format to other ISI indexes except in cases where titles are uninformative. The indexers "enrich" these titles by adding key words and phrases.

AHCI is available online only through BRS.

INDEX TO SCIENTIFIC AND TECHNICAL PROCEEDINGS (ISTP) (Philadelphia: Institute for Scientific Information, 1978-   ) covers the literally thousands of scientific meetings that take place around the world each year, approximately three-fourths of which publish some record of the papers presented. Before ISTP began, this valuable body of literature was all but inaccessible to the researcher. This index covers not only the conference proceedings as general titles but the individual papers contained in them as well. Although ISTP is similar in format to the other ISI indexes, due to the nature of the materials indexed, there are some important differences.

The indexing begins with a category index that groups the proceedings by broad categories such as "chemistry" or "cancer" or "mycology" or "optics." The number given after each title refers to the next section, Contents of Proceedings. Here each proceedings is arranged chronologically by accession number and the papers they contain are listed as they are on the title page of the published document. Complete bibliographical information is given for each proceedings entry and the page number for each individual paper is also indicated.

After the contents of proceedings section there are a series of indexes. The first indexes by author or editor the proceedings entries and all the individual papers. Up to nine editors are indexed for each proceedings. Then the sponsors of the conferences are indexed and finally the meeting locations. All of these indexes refer the researcher to the proper document through the accession numbers in the Contents of Proceedings.

The titles of the proceedings and individual papers are formed into a permuterm subject index exactly like those of other ISI publications. ISTP has a corporate index just as do SCI and SSCI. The in-depth indexing applied to this select group of materials has resulted in excellent coverage of a once neglected resource.

ISI Publications

ISI publications have a wide variety of uses other than the traditional bibliographic search. Because they are so current and so meticulously done they are extremely useful for finding the addresses of practicing scientists. They are much more up-to-date and reliable than some of the more traditional sources of this information.

Researchers can identify areas of concentration or key personnel in a field by scanning the corporate index for selected institutions.

Using the citation index the researcher can trace the use and development of a specific test or procedure or a particular school of thought simply by looking to see who cited the definitive article, and by checking the citing references for relevant works.

The ISI indexes are the most powerful print tools available to the researcher. They enable him/her to search literally thousands of journals representing dozens of fields quickly and efficiently. Researchers can also search backwards from the present by subject using the latest terminology and forwards to the present from a point in the past represented by a definitive paper.

Conclusion

All of the advantages and features of the various indexes discussed indicate their power and usefulness. Learning to use these indexes requires an investment of time and patience on the part of the user, but the information rewards are well worth that investment.

The indexes and abstracts discussed in this chapter should serve to introduce the researcher to the many tools available and to some of the more sophisticated uses of these tools. Library users should be aware that there are dozens of indexes and abstracts available which deal with virtually any subject that can be named. The choice of index depends on the project being researched, and here again the reference librarian can be helpful in making the correct decision.

6

Online Resources

The term "online resources" refers to the vast collection of data accessible by computer that is available to the modern researcher. Almost every major print bibliographic resource has a counterpart online. In effect, companies (database vendors) lease or purchase the magnetic tapes that are used to generate the print indexes, abstracts, directories, and other reference tools from the publishers (database producers). The tapes are loaded according to the vendor's software and are made available to the general public as databases. With a reasonable investment in equipment the researcher can access a database service and the online resources. The various database vendors are discussed in some detail later in this chapter.

Libraries provide an alternative access point to online resources. Most of them now offer database services through one or more of the commercial vendors. The library trains members of its staff as search analysts who then interact with the systems on behalf of the library's patrons. Although libraries ordinarily charge for these services it is usually less expensive than the researcher's own searching.

A detailed discussion of searching techniques and computer equipment is outside the scope of this book; however, there are a number of excellent publications on the subject. One of the most complete references about all aspects of online information resources is THE EXECUTIVE'S GUIDE TO ONLINE INFORMATION SERVICES by Ryan E. Hoover (White Plains, N.Y.: Knowledge Industry Publications, Inc., 1984). Mr. Hoover covers the basics as well as some more sophisticated aspects of online information retrieval. He presupposes no previous knowledge of the subject and even provides a glossary of terms to help the fledgling researcher. Numerous tables and charts help to explain and list different kinds of databases or vendors. The many figures help to elucidate and supplement the complicated text. This is an excellent starting place for any busy person who is interested in tapping into the world of online information resources. The person who can read only one title should seriously consider Hoover's book. (See Appendix II for additional references in a short, annotated bibliography on computer searching.) All the database vendors offer special training classes and refresher courses at reasonable fees. Available equipment is constantly changing and improving but the prospective searcher needs only a terminal (either visual display and/or printer), a telephone, and a modem which connects the terminal to the telephone and in turn to the main computer in which the database is stored. Commercial vendors provide the researcher with a password to enter any of the databases offered by that vendor.

Database Vendors

The three major commercial vendors of databases are DIALOG Information Services, Inc. (DIALOG), Bibliographic Retrieval Service, Inc. (BRS), and WILSONLINE, the online versions of the H. W. Wilson Co., indexes. All of these are accessible to the general public and all have a wide variety of databases. There are major differences in the software used to access them and major differences in the cost to the searcher from vendor to vendor and from database to database.

DIALOG is the largest of these with over 200 databases or files available for searching. The developer of DIALOG, Lockheed Missiles and Space Company, was also the first company to begin online bibliographic retrieval. Their available databases range from LABOR STATISTICS done by the U.S. Bureau of Labor Statistics to SCISEARCH, the online version of SCIENCE CITATION INDEX. DIALOG also provides some informational databases such as the ENCYCLOPEDIA OF ASSOCIATIONS which corresponds to the print tool of the same name, and which is discussed in greater detail in Chapter 10, Interest Groups and Networks. Services like PREDICASTS, Inc., produce a number of files for DIALOG that provide up-to-date information on technical, business, or economic forecasts as well as a file of 500 time series on the U.S. which contain historical data since 1957, called PTS U.S. TIME SERIES.

DIALOG also has a special program called the Classroom Instruction Program through which certain databases are made available at greatly reduced rates to classes and other educational groups.

DIALOG has no start-up fee. Charges are based only on the amount of time used on the computer and the citations printed plus a small telecommunications charge. Educational institutions are sometimes eligible for special contracts as are those who use large amounts of computer time each month.

BRS was established in 1976 and, with over eighty files, has fewer databases than does DIALOG. However, some databases which are unique to BRS are valuable resources. The EIGHTH MENTAL MEASUREMENTS YEARBOOK and its updates are online as MMYD. This file contains factual information on over a thousand psychological and educational tests in English. It is updated monthly. Another file is not only unique to BRS but is quite different in format from most online files. SUPE or SUPERINDEX contains millions of searchable "back of the book" index entries and page references to key reference books from twenty prominent scientific, medical, and engineering publishers. New titles and publishers are constantly being added to this file.

In addition to the online database service BRS offers individually developed software for in-house databases and library catalogs. BRS has also developed another search service option, BRS AFTER DARK. From 6:00 p.m. to midnight BRS files are available for a small fraction of the cost during the day. BRS AFTER DARK is accessed through a special user-friendly software system which is easier for the non-specialist to use. BRS has a subscription fee which entitles the subscriber to a number of hours of computer time for each billing period. Further charges are negotiated according to use; the more time used, the lower the price for computer time.

BRS also has two new programs, EDUCATOR and INSTRUCTOR. The former is designed for educators in the kindergarten through twelfth grade setting. At $18.00 per hour plus telecommunications and a $75.00 start-up fee EDUCATOR is considerably cheaper than normal BRS service. It covers a full range of databases with special emphasis on those which would be most useful to educators.

INSTRUCTOR was designed to assist in teaching online search techniques to students from elementary school level to graduate. Users pay only $15.00 per hour plus telecommunications for actual teaching time online and access to over seventy databases. Subscriptions include twelve passwords and a copy of the *User's Workbook*.

WILSONLINE is the online arm of H. W. Wilson Company, one of the most respected names in information retrieval. They also publish the print versions of a number of indexes, including READER'S GUIDE TO PERIODICAL LITERATURE and BUSINESS PERIODICALS INDEX. All of the "Wilson" indexes available in print are available online through WILSONLINE. Subscribers may prepay a prescribed amount which entitles them to a certain number of searches per year or they may pay only for computer time used. Even with the $150.00 per year licensing fee WILSONLINE is still one of the cheapest means of online information retrieval and the only access to the "Wilson" indexes online.

Another vendor, INFORMATION ACCESS COMPANY, produces both online databases and stand-alone systems for libraries. NATIONAL NEWS-PAPER INDEX and MAGAZINE INDEX are available both as microfilm indexes and as online files through BRS and DIALOG. InfoTrac and InfoTracII are optical disc (CD-ROM) reference systems which cover general periodical literature.

Many vendors offer several versions of user-friendly software and/or services, which allows researchers to directly access the major database vendors. These packages are written for microcomputers and enable the user to search using plain English instead of complicated system specific commands. In other words, it is not necessary to learn the software commands and parameters for each system; the user-friendly software overrides the systems. Some of these programs also have the capability of organizing the searcher's retrieval into a personal work-file that is also searchable. Others massage the retrieval into a tailor-made bibliographic format which can then be searched by key word or author.

Advantages of Computer Searching

Using one or more of these search services to develop a bibliography has tremendous advantages. Great quantities of material can be searched in a very short time compared to the time needed to manually search the indexes and abstracts for a particular topic. Online searching is also more flexible and more powerful. When searching manually the researcher must rely on the vocabulary or indexing provided by that service. Some of the indexing and abstracting tools assign relevant subject terms to each article they process, making that citation accessible through each of these assigned vocabulary terms. Terms are chosen from a thesaurus or controlled vocabulary list to ensure consistency of indexing. In many cases there are only two avenues of access, author and subject. Using the computer the researcher can search using this controlled vocabulary and, in addition, words which are likely to appear in the title or abstract. The researcher can also search using the author's affiliation or the title of the journal in which the article appears or any combination of the above. Some databases have dozens of access points for searching. An online reference from PSYCHINFO (PSY-CHOLOGICAL ABSTRACTS online) illustrates this.

Because comprehensive bibliographies are so easily acquired and updated researchers need not stockpile such documents. They can be generated and updated quickly as needed. In addition, computer-generated bibliographies cover the most recent literature and can be updated more often, sometimes even daily. The online version of an index or abstract is usually more current than the print product. Some databases are updated weekly or even daily. Finally, the researcher does not need to be near a major library to access the literature. Several commercial database vendors provide document de-

Illustration 6.1
PSYCHINFO Record

```
 1/5/28
58-12002
  Collaborative effect of networking: Theory, practice and dynamics.
  Ferrie, John
  U Massachusetts
  Dissertation Abstracts International,  1976 Mar Vol 36(9-B) 4663-4664
  Journal Announcement: 5806
  Language: ENGLISH  Document Type: JOURNAL ARTICLE
  Descriptors:    COOPERATION;    INTERGROUP    DYNAMICS;    ORGANIZATIONS;
COMMUNITY SERVICES; MENTAL HEALTH PROGRAMS
  Identifiers:  theory  &  practice  & dynamics, collaborative effect of
networking, helping-service agencies
  Section    Headings:    3300    (TREATMENT    AND    PREVENTION);    3650
 (ORGANIZATIONAL BEHAVIOR & JOB SATISFACTION)
```

Source: PSYCHINFO, file 11, DIALOG. These citations are reprinted with permission (fee paid) of the American Psychological Association, publisher of *Psychological Abstacts* and the PsychINFO Database (Copyright © 1987 by the American Psychological Association), and may not be reproduced without its prior permission.

livery services which make the online resources more satisfying (although possibly more expensive) than the local library.

Most database vendors offer current awareness services. For a set fee they will automatically run a search formulated to the researcher's specifications against the new material being added to a particular database with each update. For instance, ISI will pull together all the articles which have certain words chosen by the searcher and send a printout each week which is called an ASCA (Automatic Subject Citation Alert) search.

Disadvantages of Computer Searching

Although online searching is a powerful tool the researcher should be aware of the disadvantages of its use. First, there is sometimes a lack of available information. Most databases extend back to the mid–1960s at the earliest. There are a few exceptions: COMPREHENSIVE DISSERTATION ABSTRACTS goes back to 1861 and MAGAZINE INDEX goes back to 1959. Second, there are only a few databases that cover materials outside business, the sciences, and the social sciences. This can be a drawback for some areas of research. Third, as with any mechanical device, there are always systems failures to contend with and the systems may be unavailable when the researcher needs them most. Fourth, computer-generated bibliographies can also be expensive. Some databases cost as much as $300.00 per hour spent online plus charges for each citation printed, and telecommunications. While not every database is this expensive each project should be evaluated as to the cost effectiveness of using online services.

Consulting with a local reference librarian may provide added insights as to the feasibility of applying online searching capabilities to a particular information retrieval situation.

Other Considerations for Using Online Resources

In the decision to use computer search services the researcher should consider certain factors. First, is the topic to be searched one-dimensional? That is, is it built around one well-defined idea such as solar power? If so, then a manual search of the technical and scientific literature through SCIENCE CITATION INDEX or APPLIED SCIENCE AND TECHNOLOGY INDEX might be more appropriate and certainly less expensive. In any case, a perusal of several print indexes is always useful before going online as it helps the researcher know what to expect from a computer search. Online files are indexed in much greater depth than hard copy and generally cover several years per file, thus they can generate large numbers of citations if the requester is not careful to be specific.

Illustration 6.2

Comparison of PSYCHINFO Record and Record from Psychological Abstracts

Source: PSYCHINFO, file 11, DIALOG.

1/5/24
67-06753

Low-cost microcomputer networking: How to get high throughput on a low budget.

Reed, Adam V.; Lewart, Daniel; Schneider, Linda H.
New School for Social Research, Graduate Faculty of Social & Political Science

Behavior Research Methods & Instrumentation, 1981 Apr Vol 13(2) 221-226 CODEN: BRMIAC ISSN: 00057878

Journal Announcement: 6704

Language: ENGLISH Document Type: JOURNAL ARTICLE

A low-cost, high-throughput laboratory data acquisition and experiment control system may be configured by using a star network architecture with a low-cost microcomputer as network controller and 1 or more microprocessor-based single-board controllers as satellites. A network of this type using Apple II microcomputer as main node and up to 7 KIM-1 microcontrollers as satellites is described, and its development is discussed in detail. (4 ref)

Descriptors: EXPERIMENTAL LABORATORIES (18580); COMPUTER APPLICATIONS (10900); DATA COLLECTION (13005); EXPERIMENTATION (18650)

Identifiers: low-cost microcomputer network, high-throughput laboratory data acquisition & experiment control

Section Headings: 2160 (RESEARCH METHODS & APPARATUS & COMPUTER APPLICATIONS)

Illustration 6.2 continued.

From: PSYCHOLOGICAL ABSTRACTS. Washington, D.C.: American Psychological Association, 1982, volume 67, abstract number 6753.

6753. **Reed, Adam V.; Lewart, Daniel & Schneider, Linda H.** (New School for Social Research, Graduate Faculty of Social & Political Science) **Low-cost microcomputer networking: How to get high throughput on a low budget.** *Behavior Research Methods & Instrumentation,* 1981(Apr), Vol 13(2), 221–226. —A low-cost, high-throughput laboratory data acquisition and experiment control system may be configured by using a star network architecture with a low-cost microcomputer as network controller and 1 or more microprocessor-based single-board controllers as satellites. A network of this type using Apple II microcomputer as main node and up to 7 KIM-1 microcontrollers as satellites is described, and its development is discussed in detail. (4 ref)

Looking through a print index can also help the researcher to define his topic more specifically. In addition, familiarity with the print product is always helpful in online searching as they are simply two very similar versions of the same tool.

Research projects that are based on the juxtaposition of several ideas are usually more appropriate for a computer search of the literature as are topics that do not conform to the controlled vocabulary of print tools. Verifying incomplete or incorrect citations is usually much more cost effective to do online.

If online searching is done through a search intermediary the researcher must learn to trust the search analyst and must offer assistance by clearly stating the search request. The more the intermediary knows about the researcher's project the better the search will be. As with any technical skill some of these searchers are more skilled than others. The researcher should find a good analyst who understands the research project and stick to that person. If the same analyst is used over and over the researcher doesn't have to re-invent the wheel by completely restating a search request each time a search is needed during the course of the project. Search analysts are usually well trained and highly skilled and can be depended on to provide the researcher with an acceptable retrieval at the lowest possible cost.

It is important to communicate to the search intermediary the reason for the search and to distinguish between high precision and high recall searches. In what specialists call "high precision" for example, the search results should be close to 100 percent on target. That is, every citation received should be relevant. In "high recall" on the other hand, the search results will be larger but not all citations are completely on target. High recall is desirable when the search results need to be comprehensive and some peripherally related articles are retrieved in order to ensure that all the needed citations are found.

If researchers are planning on doing a lot of online searching it might be practical to examine the various online systems with an eye to obtaining their own equipment and attending one of the database vendor's training seminars. Otherwise, taking advantage of the local library's services may be more in accordance with their time and budgetary constraints. Many public and university libraries offer online services to the general public. Inquiries will not only offer details of the services offered but will usually provide a cost estimate as well.

Conclusion

Online resources are a gold mine of information for the researcher. They make available a wealth of material in a short time for a reasonable cost but they are not a panacea for all research problems. A thorough knowledge of print tools shows that online resources are merely a technological extension of indexing and abstracting services. Compiling a bibliography by whatever means is only the beginning in understanding a subject, but that beginning can often be facilitated through the use of online resources.

7

Government Agencies and Officials

Information about government agencies and officials can be especially useful to researchers interested in influencing the future. Although this information is fairly readily available, it is often overlooked because it is not accessed in the same ways as books and journals are. This chapter sets forth a few simple procedures and some useful secondary sources and services which provide access to government policies and personnel on the local, state, and national levels.

State and Local Agencies and Officials

Although municipal and state agencies and officials are not as well documented as those on the federal level there are several sources of information available to researchers.

The simplest way to find the names and telephone numbers for local and state agencies is to look in the telephone directory. Larger phone books have special blue government pages which list all levels of government. Local organizations like the Chamber of Commerce and the League of Women Voters can also be helpful in this respect. Finally, the local public library usually has this sort of information available in a specially prepared file at the reference desk.

Public and academic libraries often have telephone directories from other locations and these can be used to identify officials or contact agencies in another area. There are also special directories such as the MUNICIPAL/ COUNTY EXECUTIVE DIRECTORY (edited by Nancy Cahill. Washington, D.C.: Carroll Publishing Company, 1986) which is published annually. Only those municipalities with a population of 25,000 or more are included. This is really two separate books bound together, the Municipal Executive Directory and the County Executive Directory which are arranged in the same manner. Each has three sections: an executive listing, an organizational listing, and a geographical listing. There are also some special features such as an area code map and a listing of national municipal associations.

Carroll Publishing Company also publishes a very similar reference book called FEDERAL/STATE EXECUTIVE DIRECTORY (edited by Nancy Cahill and Pauline G. Green. Washington, D.C.: Carroll Publishing Company, 1986). Instead of a geographic listing this directory has a keyword subject index. A third Carroll publication is also worthy of comment, the FEDERAL EXECUTIVE DIRECTORY (edited by Nancy Cahill. Washington, D.C.: Carroll Publishing Company), which is updated six times a year instead of annually like the other Carroll directories mentioned above. Its format is essentially the same as the FEDERAL/STATE EXECUTIVE DIRECTORY.

Federal Agencies and Officials

In 1966 Congress passed the Freedom of Information Act. Under this law, any identifiable records of the administrative agencies in the executive branch of the federal government must be released if requested. There are, of course, some exemptions to the act. These include Presidential papers and classified documents, among others.

The act requires only that the requestor write a letter identifying the materials desired. It is not necessary to state why the materials are wanted. Some departments charge for the materials requested but they are prohibited by law from charging more than the actual cost of searching for and copying documents.

The Freedom of Information Act is discussed in great detail in an excellent reference source called INFORMATION U.S.A. by Matthew Lesko (New York: Viking Press, 1986). This book discusses all of the sources for information in Washington, D.C., and in so doing provides a comprehensive guide to all of the departments of all the branches of the federal government. In addition to a large directory section, INFORMATION U.S.A. has a "Sampler" section, which describes information available without charge from the government regarding health, buying an automobile and several other topics. This section also contains a list of "quasi-official" agencies like the Smithsonian. With both a detailed table of contents and an extensive index finding specific information is extremely easy. Addresses and telephone numbers as well as a brief description of its purpose are given for each departmental division. This book gives the most comprehensive and detailed treatment of the various agencies of the federal government on the market today.

Another source, the GUIDE TO CURRENT AMERICAN GOVERN-MENT (Washington, D.C.: Congressional Quarterly) is published twice a year and describes the activities of Congress; politics in general, including elections and campaigns; and covers the activities of the executive branch, the Supreme Court, and lobbyists. The appendixes cover various diverse topics such as a glossary of Congressional terms, a description of how a bill becomes a law, and a reference guide. Because this source is published every six months it is an excellent tool for monitoring issues which affect various political interest groups and for detecting changes in the political climate. The section designed for lobbyists covers events affecting political interest groups and group activities which affect political events. In addition, it can be useful to review back issues of the GUIDE TO CURRENT AMER-ICAN GOVERNMENT in order to identify past trends and issues.

WORKING ON THE SYSTEM: A COMPREHENSIVE MANUAL FOR CITIZEN ACCESS TO FEDERAL AGENCIES (edited by James R. Michael. New York: Basic Books, 1974) concentrates on the interaction between public or citizen interest groups and federal agencies. It provides thorough discussions on additional information sources about agencies and how to deal with them. Of special importance to interest groups is the chapter on the Freedom of Information Act. Knowledge of this law is essential to deal effectively with agencies. WORKING ON THE SYSTEM contains a good discussion of group organizational resources as well as appendixes which include a directory of consumer groups and consumer press lists, and sample letter and rule-making formats. The major portion of the book deals with thirteen separate agencies explaining each one's procedures, organization, and the scope of its activities. Although not as readable as HOW YOU CAN INFLUENCE CONGRESS, which is discussed later in this chapter, WORKING ON THE SYSTEM provides the detailed information necessary for working with the bureaucracies of the agencies listed.

One final reference is noted because of its usefulness and availability in most libraries. The UNITED STATES GOVERNMENT MANUAL (Washington, D.C.: Office of the Federal Register, 1935–   ) is the official handbook of the federal government and provides comprehensive information on all three branches of government. This book focuses on the programs and activities of federal agencies and describes the organization, purpose, function, programs, and key personnel of most governmental agencies. There are also brief descriptions of some quasi-official agencies and organizations such as the Legal Services Corporation.

THE FEDERAL REGISTER (Washington, D.C.: Office of the Federal Register, National Archives and Records Services, General Services Administration, 1936-   ) is published daily and contains federal agency notifications and regulation proposals, changes and amendments, as well as other legal documents of the executive branch. Notices of public meetings and government requirements for regulated area standards such as those for food and drugs or the environment are included. Because of its complexity, educational workshops on using THE FEDERAL REGISTER are regularly scheduled in Washington and may be scheduled in other cities by special arrangement. Many libraries subscribe to this publication and, given a specific citation from another source, it is fairly easy to look up that citation in THE FEDERAL REGISTER.

The CODE OF FEDERAL REGULATIONS (Washington, D.C.: National Archives, 1949-   ) is the annual compilation of regulations published daily in THE FEDERAL REGISTER plus additional regulations which are still in effect. The compilation is arranged into fifty titles representing broad subject areas. It is revised once a year and issued on a staggered quarterly basis. At the back of the volumes, the "Finding Aids" section alphabetically lists the agencies in that volume with corresponding subtitle and chapter assignments. The CODE OF FEDERAL REGULATIONS provides a comprehensive source of general and permanent federal regulations. For many purposes, it can be used instead of THE FEDERAL REGISTER and as it is indexed, specific regulations are easier to find.

Federal Information Centers are located nationwide in most large cities and toll free numbers provide connections to cities where there is no office. These centers are clearinghouses for referral services to information sources in the federal government. At times, they can also provide city and county referrals. When a Federal Information Center receives a request for information, it either supplies the information or refers the caller to the appropriate agency or office. Many large public libraries provide similar referral services and act as a depository for state and federal documents. In addition, their reference staff will answer questions concerning all aspects of government and its operations.

Congress

The United States Congress is the most pervasive of any arm of the federal government and its activities are extremely well documented in print and online sources.

There are several widely available references which provide information on various elected and appointed federal officials. The first of these, the CONGRESSIONAL DIRECTORY (Washington, D.C.: U.S. Government Printing Office, 1865-   ), is the official directory of the United States Congress. It provides an alphabetical listing of members in the House and Senate, their addresses, the names of their administrative and legislative assistants, and brief biographies which include a description of each member's district. It also contains a committee list and each member's committee assignments. In addition, this directory lists departments both of the executive branch and of independent agencies and their top personnel. There is also some statistical information concerning legislation but no description of duties or responsibilities. It is primarily a "Capitol Hill" telephone directory and is as easy to use as any telephone book.

The CONGRESSIONAL STAFF DIRECTORY by Charles B. Brownson (Mt. Vernon, N.Y.: Congressional Staff Directory, 1959-   ) is virtually the same book as the CONGRESSIONAL DIRECTORY discussed in the preceding paragraph except that it is privately published. One of its interesting features is the color-coded index in the front of the book for quick access to the content. It covers the state delegations, the Senate, joint committees and staff, the House, and a city and town listing of congressional districts and members. The key personnel of executive department and agencies, as well as listings of congressional staff and an index of individuals are all part of this book.

The following publications represent only a few of the information sources published by the Congressional Quarterly Press.   All of their publications are excellent references on all aspects of government. The GUIDE TO CONGRESS by Robert A. Diamond and Patricia Ann O'Connor (3d ed., Washington, D.C.: Congressional Quarterly Press, 1983) is an overview of the political process from the congressional perspective. It covers the history of Congress, congressional powers, procedures, housing, and support. The table of contents furnishes an overall view of the book's scope and a quick access to its major sections. This valuable tool also includes a subject index to charts, tables, and summaries, as well as selected bibliographies and footnotes to additional references. CONGRESS AND THE NATION (Washington, D.C.: Congressional Quarterly Press, 1945-   ) is published every four years and records the government activities for one presidential term. It provides a good perspective of the way issues emerge and are resolved within the political process.

The major publication of Congressional Quarterly Press is the CONGRESSIONAL QUARTERLY WEEKLY REPORT (Washington, D.C.: Congressional Quarterly Press, 1946-   ). It contains reports and analyses of all the major issues and legislation considered in Congress during the previous week. The most important feature of the WEEKLY REPORT is the voting compilation which describes the bill and how members and parties voted.

The Congressional Information Service (CIS) publishes three major reference works, each with its own separate index and abstract volumes and documents on microfiche. Two of these, the STATISTICAL REFERENCE INDEX and the AMERICAN STATISTICS INDEX will be discussed in more detail in Chapter 8, Government Documents. The third, CONGRESSIONAL INFORMATION SERVICE/INDEX (Washington, D.C.: Congressional Information Service, 1970-   ) indexes all the working papers, reports and other documentation generated by Congress with the exception of the CONGRESSIONAL RECORD.

CONGRESSIONAL INFORMATION SERVICE/INDEX is a system of comprehensive indexing that provides access to an accompanying collection of microfiche. Thus the researcher can identify a committee hearing or congressional report and then actually see a microfiche copy of the document. Since most of this material is not available anywhere outside Washington, CIS/INDEX has been a boon to researchers who need to follow the activities of the Congress. The collection of documents is updated monthly and indexed by subject, title, bill number, report number, and document number. This resource is available online through DIALOG.

The CONGRESSIONAL RECORD (Washington, D.C.: Government Printing Office, 1873-   ) prints the daily proceedings and debates of Congress in their entirety. It is organized into three parts: the daily CONGRESSIONAL RECORD with separate House and Senate volume, the DAILY DIGEST outlining chamber and committee actions, and the RESUME OF CONGRESSIONAL ACTIVITY which outlines all legislative business in both chambers. A bound set is published yearly in fifteen to twenty parts with a separate index. Finding a specific hearing or a particular member's comments in the CONGRESSIONAL RECORD can be very difficult and time consuming. However, the CONGRESSIONAL RECORD is the only source for determining *exactly* what happened to a bill in the House or Senate. This day-by-day record of what goes on in Congress includes some remarks not actually made on the floor of the House or Senate. Members may insert remarks into the record in a section called "Extension of Remarks." These are added to elaborate on the issue of a vote and are not infrequently written by a staff member for the benefit of the constituents back home.

Commerce Clearing House is an old and respected publisher of legal books and looseleaf subscription services. The ELECTRONIC LEGISLATIVE SEARCH SYSTEM (ELSS) is a natural outgrowth of their previous publishing activities. ELSS is an online system dedicated to the tracking of state and federal legislation.

State legislative activity is loaded as soon as it is reported by the state legislature. Speed of reporting varies from state to state with some states reporting within a few days. The files report only the current legislative session's activities, the previous session's file is kept online for a short time and then deleted. ELSS can be searched by subject, bill number, sponsor, and date. At the federal level ELSS reports activity as published in the CONGRESSIONAL RECORD and provides next-day access to Congressional activities.

This system offers services on a number of levels ranging from simple online access to the delivery of copies of all bills, committee hearings, amendments, and final legislation for pre-selected states or subject areas. At a *minimum* cost of $3000.00 a year ELSS is expensive, but a unique service like this one can be invaluable to a researcher or interest group attempting to monitor legislation on the state or federal level.

There is another online federal tracking system called LEGI-SLATE which began in 1980. This system is menu-driven and therefore very easy to search. It reports federal legislative actions as published in the CONGRESSIONAL RECORD from the start of the 96th Congress in 1979. In 1981 the company began tracking regulatory announcements published in the FEDERAL REG-ISTER as well. One of the database's strongest points is that it is updated daily.

LEGI-SLATE is expensive with a minimum monthly fee of over $400.00 and an hourly rate of $195.00. Copies of bills, hearings or other documents can be requested by electronic mail for a nominal fee.

HOW YOU CAN INFLUENCE CONGRESS: THE COMPLETE HANDBOOK FOR THE CITIZEN LOBBYIST by George Alderson and Everett Sentman (New York: E. P. Dutton, 1979) is an excellent guide to lobbying activities. It enumerates specific tactics, explains how to communicate with officials, and contains selected bibliographies for specific skill development. This book is well organized and easy to read and the table of contents makes referral to specific topics quick and easy. More information about lobbyists and special interest groups is included in Chapter 9, Interest Groups and Networks.

Conclusion

General information about government agencies and officials is readily available in most libraries. Many larger public and academic libraries have extensive collections of reference books, telephone directories as well as the FEDERAL REGISTER, CONGRESSIONAL RECORD, and the CODE OF FEDERAL REGULATIONS. In addition, most reference departments keep a special file on local officeholders and agencies. Of course, the use of all of these is free to library patrons. Between these print tools and the online resources generally available at reasonable rates the average researcher can usually find more than enough information about government agencies and officials.

8

Government Documents

All of the various agencies and officials discussed in the previous chapter publish documents. These publications range from pamphlets of a few pages to multi-volume reports. Although government documents can be more difficult to find than some other types of resources, they contain much unique information and are usually worth the trouble. Many times governments are the only organizational structure interested in a particular problem or large enough to provide the resources and framework for the study of that problem. This chapter discusses government documents and their access on four levels: local, state, United States, and international.

Local Documents

Documents published by cities or consortia of cities can best be accessed by contacting the city or consortium in question. Most libraries have collections of telephone directories which can provide addresses for city governing bodies or consortia. In addition, the local Chamber of Commerce office has directories which include all the other chambers of commerce in the country. These organizations generally have information regarding governing bodies and agencies in their locale. If this approach proves unsuccessful the researcher can attempt to retrieve the document through a nearby public or academic library. Libraries frequently serve as informal depositories of local documents and many libraries make a special effort to provide users with access to publications of this nature. These libraries can be identified by using the AMERICAN LIBRARY DIRECTORY (39th ed., edited by Jacques Cattell Press. New York: R. R. Bowker, 1986), which is a listing of all the libraries in the United States. Entries are arranged alphabetically by state and then by city and give brief descriptions of the library as well as its address and telephone number.

Larger public and academic libraries offer a slightly different approach to finding locally produced documents. Many of them subscribe to reference works which provide information on the local level. One of the most important is INDEX TO CURRENT URBAN DOCUMENTS (Westport, Conn.: Greenwood Press, 1972-   ). This index covers municipal government reports, studies, and special publications and makes them available on microfiche. Most of the documents are concerned with public affairs and are indexed by geographic location and subject.

THE MUNICIPAL YEAR BOOK (MYB) (Washington, D.C.: International City Management Association, 1934-   ) is the compilation of the results of a survey taken from local government officials. The MYB is organized into six sections: local government profiles, the intergovernmental dimension, personnel issues, management issues and trends, directories, and references.

The directory section is especially valuable as it guides the researcher to sources beyond the MYB. The state municipal leagues, state agencies for community affairs, and individuals in municipalities, countries, and regional councils are extremely useful for the exchange of information and for networking. The last section, references, provides the user with an extensive bibliography on municipal management and government from the latest books and periodicals.

Control Data Corporation has developed a computer-based information retrieval system called LOGIN (Local Government Information Network). This system has three interrelated functions. It provides online information retrieval and it enables members to add records to the database. In addition, it allows the transmitting and reading of communication among users, an electronic mail service.

LOGIN differs from most commercial databases in that its users supply the database records. Each record describes a problem and the technique which was used to address the problem. The name and address of a contact person are supplied with each record. LOGIN's marketing has thus far been directed toward planners rather than information specialists and consequently has concentrated on the system's electronic mail functions. However, with almost 30,000 records it has become a valuable, if untapped, information retrieval source. Plans have been made to enhance the LOGIN database with the addition of INDEX TO CURRENT URBAN DOCUMENTS, discussed earlier in this chapter.

This system is not readily accessible to the casual user. Control Data Corporation charges a large annual fee ($3,000 at this writing). This includes all documentation and 200 hours of online time. Credits of $40 each are given for approved records submitted by the users.

While the LOGIN system is not, in the strictest sense, a government document, it serves the same purpose: it provides a record of the workings of government.

State Documents

On the state level documents are more carefully preserved and collected. As a general rule the state library is designated a full depository for its state's publications and there are usually several other partial depositories around the state. Full depositories are required by law to keep and make accessible all of the documents published by the geopolitical area they represent, while partial depositories receive and keep only the documents that they request.

Access to state documents is greatly facilitated by books like David W. Parish's STATE GOVERNMENT PUBLICATIONS (2d. ed., Littleton, Colo.: Libraries Unlimited, Inc., 1981). This book provides a bibliography of document sources, state by state, as well as a comprehensive list of state agencies that are responsible for publishing and disseminating documents.

The Government Documents Round Table of the American Library Association has produced a microfiche collection called the DOCUMENTS ON DOCUMENTS COLLECTION. A user's guide to this collection of documents is available from Lane, Fertitta, Lane, and Tullos, a law firm (P.O. Box 3335, Baton Rouge, Louisiana, 70821), for $3.00. The collection gathers together documents produced from 1973 to 1979 by documents distribution centers from all fifty states. These documents were originally produced for the administrators of document depository programs and other state employees. They are arranged by state and category and, conversely, then by category and state. The categories include bibliographies and reference tools, legislation and legal materials, manuals, procedural guidelines, studies, surveys, and workshops. This extremely valuable project has resulted in a core collection of state documents which can in turn lead to many other documents published in all fifty states.

The 1973–1979 collection of documents is currently available from ERIC as a microfiche collection with a print guide. The current collection, from 1980 on, is being circulated as paper copies. It is available, with a guide, on interlibrary loan from Grace G. Moore, Recorder of Documents, Louisiana State Library (P.O. Box 131, Baton Rouge, Louisiana, 70821).

The accessibility and organization of state documents varies from state to state. Some states have well organized document distribution systems and others maintain very little control over their publications. While the bibliographic tools mentioned earlier in this chapter do make state documents more manageable there are still many problems associated with their use. If state documents are needed for a project then the state library of the state in question should be contacted in addition to using the resources mentioned in this chapter. State documents are also indexed by the STATISTICAL REFERENCE INDEX which is discussed later in this chapter.

United States Government Documents

There are three major access routes to documents published by the U.S. government: MONTHLY CATALOG, NATIONAL TECHNICAL INFORMATION SERVICE, and the Congressional Information Services indexes. All of these indexes provide different types of coverage for U.S. documents. Although there is some overlap between them, no *single* index exists for *all* U.S. government publications.

The MONTHLY CATALOG (Washington, D.C.: Government Printing Office, 1895-   ) comes the closest to being an overall index to these documents. It has gone through a number of incarnations in coverage and format during the past century. Today it serves as an index for all the documents sold by the Superintendent of Documents, both those for official use and those which are sent to depository libraries. There are two full depository libraries for each state and many, many partial depositories. A list of the full depositories is located at the front of each issue of the MONTHLY CATALOG.

Documents are indexed by author, title, subject, series/report numbers, stock number, and title key word. The monthly volumes are cumulated semi-annually and annually. Complete instructions for using the index and ordering documents can be found at the beginning of each issue. The greatest strength of the MONTHLY CATALOG lies in its comprehensive coverage and in-depth indexing of most of the documents published by the United States.

Researchers can also find information about government documents in the GPO SALES PUBLICATIONS REFERENCE FILE (Washington, D.C.: Government Printing Office). This microfiche catalog contains listings for all the in-print publications offered for sale by the Superintendent of Documents. It is completely revised every two months and supplemented monthly in between complete revisions.

U.S. government publications can also be obtained through the local library or they can be purchased at GPO (Government Printing Office) bookstores at various locations around the country. They can also be ordered directly from the Superintendent of Documents using the order form at the beginning of each issue of the MONTHLY CATALOG. In addition to the print version, the MONTHLY CATALOG is available online through DIALOG and BRS.

The NATIONAL TECHNICAL INFORMATION SERVICE (NTIS) is a

part of the U.S. Department of Commerce. It was established in 1970 to provide public access to the documents generated by the Department of Commerce as well as to data files and reports produced by federal agencies and their contractors. NTIS serves as a huge repository which supplies the public with millions of these documents annually. NTIS does not handle depository documents. There has been continuous wrangling between NTIS and GPO as to what agency should handle what documents; therefore, the researcher is reduced to searching both tools if he is interested in an exhaustive search of the U.S. documents literature.

Comprehensive bibliographic coverage of NTIS titles is provided through GOVERNMENT REPORTS ANNOUNCEMENTS & INDEX (GRA&I) (Springfield, Va.: National Technical Information Service, 1946–   ) which is published semi-monthly. This indexing and abstracting service provides access to NTIS documents through broad subject category, keyword, personal author name, corporate author name, contract number, grant number, report number, or NTIS order number. Complete instructions for its use are found at the beginning of each issue of GRA&I.

NTIS provides other services based on its document collection. It publishes weekly abstract newsletters in twenty-six subject categories. Abstracts are for documents recently received and these newsletters serve as an excellent means of staying abreast of the government contracting being done in these fields. Another special service of NTIS is called SRIM (Selected Research in Microfiche). SRIM is an automatic biweekly service through which the subscriber receives microfiche copies of all the documents received by NTIS in the subject areas the subscriber chooses. Instead of choosing individual documents the subscriber chooses a subject area and has a standing order with NTIS for all reports in that field that are processed through NTIS. NTIS also has available over 4,000 bibliographies with abstracts that have been prepared in anticipation of user need. All NTIS records are available online through DIALOG and BRS.

Although these two government publications provide excellent access to government documents there are a number of commercial services which also deal with U.S. government documents. One of these, AMERICAN STATISTICS INDEX (ASI) (Washington, D.C.: Congressional Information Service, 1960-   ) provides a master index to all the U.S. government publications from *any* source that provides statistical or tabular information. An accompanying set of microfiche provides the full text of all the publications indexed. The items in this collection constitute over 90 percent of all documents published by the United States.

ASI covers a broad range of documents many of which are not a part of the GPO or NTIS files and that are not available in depository libraries. Since it indexes an accompanying microfiche collection it provides the user with a wealth of immediately available statistical information. ASI is updated monthly and indexed by subject, name (includes both corporate and personal authors), categories, title, and agency report numbers. It is also available online through DIALOG.

STATISTICAL REFERENCE INDEX (SRI) (Washington, D.C.: Congressional Information Service, 1980-   ) follows the same format: extensive print indexes to a large collection of documents on microfiche. SRI covers documents which contain national and state data derived from publications other than U.S. federal government publications.

SRI is indexed by subjects and names. The names index includes the names of individuals and organizations that are subjects or authors. There is also a categories index. Here data is broken down by any of twenty categories such as state or age. Finally the documents are indexed by issuing source and by publication title.

Several publications are available free from Congressional Information Service, Inc. (4520 East-West Highway, Bethesda, Md., 20914) which describe ASI and SRI in more detail.

DATAMAP 1986: INDEX OF PUBLISHED TABLES OF STATISTICAL DATA by Jarol B. Manheim and Allison Ondrasik (Phoenix, Ariz.: Oryx Press, 1986) is an exceptionally useful bibliographic tool in the field of statistics. This single-volume work provides access to a wide variety of statistical data from twenty-nine sources. The sources include publications of the United States government, the United Nations and its agencies as well as some other public and private organizations.

DATAMAP is divided into three sections. Section I is a list of all the sources indexed, Section III is a controlled vocabulary index which refers the user to Section II, which is a reference to the sources listed in Section I. These sources range from the STATISTICAL ABSTRACT OF THE UNITED STATES to the WORLD ECONOMIC SURVEY, and most are readily available in larger public and academic libraries.

The STATISTICAL ABSTRACT OF THE UNITED STATES (106th ed., Washington, D.C.: Government Printing Office, 1987) is one of the most heavily used government documents being published. Now in its 106th annual edition, the STATISTICAL ABSTRACT OF THE UNITED STATES provides a single volume of quantitative summary statistics about the U.S. It is the standard summary of statistics on the social, political, and economic organization of the United States. Not only does it serve as a convenient volume for statistical reference but it is also a guide to other statistical publications and sources, both public and private, because all information is referenced to its original source. Tabular data covers topics from population to health and nutrition to elections to fisheries. This book is indispensable to any library's collection and a good starting point for any research question which concerns U.S. statistics.

In addition to all of its print publications the United States government has developed over 3,000 databases, many of which are available free.

Subject coverage ranges from crude oil availability to travel information to demographics. THE FEDERAL DATA BASE FINDER (Potomac, Md.: Information, USA, 1986) is a guide to all of the free and fee-based files available from the federal government.

The directory's clear, readable format divides the files into categories. Each entry includes information on the use of the database, the name and address of the office responsible for it, and the price if there is a charge for its use. There is also a separate section devoted to federal databases available through commercial vendors such as DIALOG or BRS. The databases represented in this book provide additional access to millions of documents which are published in the more traditional print format.

FEDfind: YOUR KEY TO FINDING FEDERAL GOVERNMENT INFORMATION: A DIRECTORY OF INFORMATION SOURCES, PRODUCTS, AND SERVICES by Richard J. D'Aleo (2d. ed., Springfield, Va.: ICUC Press, 1986) is a general guide to government publications. The author supplies many Superintendent of Documents numbers which help to provide easy access to most depository library collections. He also has included chapters on federal employment and the federal budget process which are especially useful. This book complements INFORMATION USA by Matthew Lesko which was discussed earlier.

USING GOVERNMENT PUBLICATIONS by Jean L. Sears and Marilyn K. Moody (Phoenix, Ariz.: Oryx Press, 1985–86) is an excellent guide to finding information in government publications. This work is published in two volumes. The first, "Searching by Subjects and Agencies," also contains introductory material about government publications in general as well as a detailed description of how search strategies are formulated and basic information about the arrangement of government documents. Each subject chapter begins with a search strategy and ends with a section on online resources and other related material.

Volume 2, "Finding Statistics and Using Special Techniques," repeats the introductory material from Volume 1 and uses the same format for its additional chapters. The first chapters cover all aspects of statistics and the second section, "Special Techniques," includes chapters on the following: historical searches, National Archives, technical reports, patents, and trademarks. Extensive indexes cover both volumes. This is one of the best descriptive tools for learning about government document access routes currently available. The search strategy format makes it especially valuable to the novice researcher.

International Documents

Documents of foreign governments and the United Nations have a much more limited access than U.S. government documents. The only readily available index to these publications is PUBLIC AFFAIRS INFORMATION

SERVICE (PAIS) which is discussed in some detail in Chapter 5, Abstracts and Indexes. Unfortunately, PAIS covers only a small portion of the total number of documents published. Some more specialized libraries may have UNDEX, United Nations Documents Index (New York: United Nations, 1970–   ), which has been published since 1970. UNDEX is issued in three series: subject index, country index, and a list of documents indexed. Another source of information on the U.N. is UNDIS, the United Nations Documentation Information System (New York: United Nations, 1974-   ), which provides information on the products and services of the U.N. One particularly useful service described is the series of indexes to resolutions and proceedings available from UNDIS. U.N. documents can be ordered through UNIPUB (1180 Avenue of the Americas, New York, N.Y. 10036) and many are available through interlibrary loan. UNIPUB also supplies catalogs listing all the documents they have in stock.

Congressional Information Service, Inc., publishes the INDEX TO INTERNATIONAL STATISTICS (IIS) (Washington, D.C.: Congressional Information Services, 1983-   ) which is similar in format to ASI and SRI which were discussed earlier in this chapter. IIS identifies and catalogs all of the statistical publications published by all the major international intergovernmental agencies. Each cataloged entry has an abstract and is indexed by subject and geographic detail. A second phase of the service is a collection of microfiche reproductions of all the documents, which accompanies the index.

Conclusion

Government documents represent a large collection of valuable research material that has only recently been made accessible to the general public. Now through new indexing and abstracting services and online files these documents can provide much needed background material. The information was always there—more sophisticated techniques of bibliographic control and retrieval have made it available to everyone.

9

Interest Groups and Networks

Organizations and individuals are useful to researchers in two ways. One, their purpose or work has an intrinsic value and those interested in that particular field can often benefit from their publications and activities. Second, they serve as contacts and access points to those who support their purpose and work. In other words, they are the key to networking.

Forming a network with like-minded individuals or organizations is a time-honored way to achieve a goal that might be impossible for the individual entities of the network to attain alone. Gaining access to established networks or forming new ones is not nearly as difficult as might be supposed. This chapter is designed to guide the researcher to several readily available sources that will help them identify the right organization or individual to contact regarding their particular interest.

There are several excellent books about networks in general and about forming networks. NETWORKING: THE FIRST REPORT AND DIRECTORY by Jessica Lipnack and Jeffrey Stamps (Garden City, N.Y.: Doubleday & Co., 1982) is both a directory and a how-to book. The first part of each chapter talks about a kind of network or networking system and the last part or guide is a list of that type of network. The first and last chapters, "Discovering Another America" and "The Art of Networking," are nuts and bolts descriptions of what makes a successful network function and how to go about starting and maintaining a network.

Lipnack and Stamps published THE NETWORKING BOOK: PEOPLE CONNECTING WITH PEOPLE by Jessica Lipnack and Jeffrey Stamps (New York: Methuen, 1986) as a revision of their 1982 book; however, the latter work is quite different in scope. It concentrates on networking in general and its theory, as well as a description of the state of networking today. The new edition contains much material on different networks, but most of it is presented in an anecdotal fashion. There is a directory of networks at the end of the book which includes addresses.

Jessica Lipnack and Jeffrey Stamps are the founders and directors of the Networking Institute, Inc. (P.O. Box 66, West Newton, Mass. 02165), which publishes the NETWORKING NEWSLETTER and NETWORKING JOURNAL.

Another book, NETWORKING by Mary Scott Welch (New York: Warner Books, 1981), is directed toward women. However, there is much information here which will be useful for anyone interested in joining an existing network or starting their own. In one particularly interesting section Welch analyzes failed networks and failed projects that could have benefited from networking.

Organizations

The chief means of identifying organizations in the United States is THE ENCYCLOPEDIA OF ASSOCIATIONS (21st ed., Detroit: Gale Research Co., 1986). This heavily used reference work is a staple part of every library's reference collection. It is published in several volumes with periodic supplements to update the information, which changes between the publication of the annual editions. Each citation includes the organization's name, address, telephone number, chief executive officer, membership size, affiliated organizations and publications, and a short paragraph that summarizes the goals of the organization. These citations are indexed alphabetically by key word from the organization's name, by geographic area, and by chief executive officer. THE ENCYCLOPEDIA OF ASSOCIATIONS is available online only through DIALOG.

A second work. NATIONAL TRADE AND PROFESSIONAL ASSOCIATIONS AND LABOR UNIONS OF THE UNITED STATES AND CANADA (22nd ed., edited by Craig Colgate, Jr., Washington, D.C.: Columbia Books, 1987), contains citations for over 6,000 organizations. It is revised annually and only cites groups which have national memberships. It is easily accessed through any of four alphabetical indexes: organization name, executive, keyword (by product, field or profession), and geographic. Each citation includes the organization's chief executive officer and his address, the size of its membership, its annual budget, and publications, if any.

The organizations described in the publications listed above publish a vast wealth of materials in the process of recording their activities and communicating special information to their membership. Standard bibliographic sources such as BOOKS IN PRINT do not list these publications and they are rarely advertised outside the organization's membership. These two factors combine to make their acquisition difficult. ASSOCIATIONS' PUBLICATIONS IN PRINT (APIP) (New York: R. R. Bowker & Co., 1984) solves many of these acquisition problems.

This relatively new reference work is a three-volume series of indexes to the publications of 3,900 associational publishers. The 104,000 titles in the 1984–85 edition are indexed in a variety of ways. The publications themselves are indexed by subject using Library of Congress headings, and by title. The publishers are indexed by subject, name, and acronym. There is also a publisher/title index in which the associations are listed alphabetically and the titles of their publications are listed alphabetically under each association. This is especially useful when the researcher is interested in reviewing the scope of an association's publications.

ASSOCIATIONS' PUBLICATIONS IN PRINT is definitive and essential. In addition to the obvious information it provides about the publications of numerous associations, it also provides information about the priorities of the organization as reflected in the subject matter of those publications. APIP is available online through BRS.

Two groups, the Chamber of Commerce and the League of Women Voters, deserve special mention in this book because of the constituencies they represent and because of the networks they have established through local, state, and national organizations. Chambers of Commerce, whether at the national, state, or local level, are a gold mine of information. Committee work is the heart of the Chamber of Commerce at any level. These committees prepare reports describing their policies, goals, and activities which can be used to determine emerging issues and trends. Unfortunately, unless there is a member willing to provide them, these committee reports can be difficult to procure.

Another excellent source to evaluate Chamber positions is each chamber's annual report. Again, acquisition of the document is usually contingent upon a member's cooperation. Many chambers also publish other documents, some of which are available free through their offices. The local Chamber of Commerce can provide the addresses of chambers in other cities.

The League of Women Voters is another organization which provides valuable information on a variety of contemporary issues. There is a nominal charge for most League materials, but some reports and pamphlets are available at no cost. The League has national, state, and local chapters, all of which sponsor and conduct public information seminars, meetings, and debates. It is an excellent starting point for information about local planning issues and political priorities in a community.

Individuals

Identifying individuals who are not elected or appointed or who are not associated with a particular organization is one of the most difficult problems facing researchers. There are several basic sources which are especially useful partly because they are so readily available. BIOGRAPHY INDEX (New York: H. W. Wilson Co., 1947-   ) is a quarterly index to biographical material that appears in books and magazines, mostly those indexed by the other Wilson publications. (See Chapter 5, Abstracts and Indexes, for a more complete description of Wilson indexes.) The familiar Wilson format includes indexes by name and profession or occupation. This is a good source for obituaries of recently deceased people. CURRENT BIOGRAPHY (New York: H. W. Wilson Co., 1940-   ) also publishes biographical information. The coverage is quite different from BIOGRAPHY INDEX in that the individual articles are longer and give a concise biographical sketch rather than just references to other sources. Only 300 to 500 people are covered in a year's time but they are usually people not covered by other, more traditional biographical sources and directories.

BIOGRAPHY MASTER INDEX, files 287 and 288 on DIALOG, has well over two million entries from more than 600 source publications. The people included in these files are scientists, celebrities, sports figures, and other prominent people, both historical and contemporary. Records include the name of the person, his/her birth (and death) date, and the source publication which provides the information.

The NATIONAL FACULTY DIRECTORY 1987 (Detroit: Gale Research Co., 1986) is an alphabetical list with addresses of over half a million members of teaching faculties at junior colleges, colleges, and universities in the United States and Canada. It is compiled and maintained from current academic catalogs and course lists and confirmed by personal questionnaires that are distributed every eighteen months. Only faculty with classroom teaching responsibilities are considered for inclusion. Since teaching faculty are a relatively transient occupational group some errors of affiliation are found, but this does serve as an important tool for locating teaching faculty.

Alternative sources of biographical information are WHO'S WHO IN AMERICA (Chicago: Marquis Who's Who, Inc., 1899-   ) and the citation indexes. WHO'S WHO IN AMERICA has been published since 1899 and is a catalog of short biographies of outstanding Americans. Candidates for inclusion are asked to fill out a data form which is submitted to a rigorous selection process. Solicitation for inclusion must come from the editors; wealth and social position are never criteria for inclusion. Selection is judged by noteworthy achievements that have proved of significant value to society.

The source indexes of all ISI publications list the affiliation and address of the first author of each article. (See Chapter 5 for a complete discussion of ISI indexes.) Sometimes this is the only information available about a person and frequently this is the person's most current address. ISI also produces WHO'S PUBLISHING IN SCIENCE. (Philadelphia: Institute for Scientific Information, 1978-   ) which is merely a compilation of all of its source index author entries and their affiliations. For this reason many libraries that subscribe to the citation indexes have chosen not to purchase WHO'S PUBLISHING IN SCIENCE in addition to the citation indexes.

Finally, the ELECTRONIC YELLOW PAGES—PROFESSIONALS (available only through DIALOG, file 502) provides online yellow-page information for professionals in insurance, real estate, medicine, law, engineering, and accounting. The database contains a full directory listing for each corporation, company, firm, or individual which includes the name and address, county name, telephone number, modified four digit Standard Industrial Classification code and office size. The data is taken from the most current yellow pages of telephone books from every part of the United States and is cross-checked and qualified using more than fifty other sources.

Lobbyists

Lobbyists are individuals who represent special interest groups and organizations to Congress in Washington or to state legislative bodies. They are important because of the power granted them by virtue of their influence with our lawmakers.

Columbia Books publishes a volume which focuses on Washington lobbyists and political action committees (PACs) called WASHINGTON REPRESENTATIVES OF AMERICAN ASSOCIATIONS AND INDUSTRY (10th ed., Washington, D.C.: Columbia Books, 1986). This directory provides a brief, but good, overview of political interest groups, their operation, membership size, and dues. It is a particularly useful reference for groups involved in analyzing the lobbying strategies of other groups because PACs are the committees responsible for distributing the campaign contributions of industries.

Other books on lobbyists and lobbying can be found at the local public library under the heading, "lobbying."

Conclusion

The sources discussed in this chapter provide a first step for building or entering networks. These access tools to information about people or organizations can be very helpful to researchers or citizens groups in that they provide a "toe hold" into the system. This "toe hold" can be the catalyst that enables the person or group to successfully tap into existing networks. It may also inspire them to create their own network using the contacts they have made.

10

Funding Sources

Organizations that need to raise funds can go about it in a number of different ways. Direct mail fundraising is a very effective tool if the organization has the resources to undertake such a campaign. Special events are another time-honored way of raising money and can be very successful. Also, contributions from wealthy individuals are usually welcome, but an organization cannot afford to depend on them for day-to-day operations. The largest source of funds for many organizations is grants; either from corporate sources, foundations, or governments. This chapter will deal with the process of obtaining grants funds from all these different sources.

Obtaining grants is a complicated process and in many instances requires the service of a professional consultant. At the very least the organization needs to be familiar with the major sources of grants and their application procedures before undertaking the actual requests for grants.

Several excellent books can be very useful to the inexperienced organization seeking grant money. One of the best is called PLAYING THE FUNDING GAME by Gregory C. Horgen (Sacramento, Calif.: Human Services Development Center, 1981). This book starts at the very beginning with advice about developing leadership within an organization, focusing especially on the board of directors. Mr. Horgen also offers a basic primer on nonprofit marketing strategies and on all kinds of fundraising. The bulk of the book however, is on grantsmanship. Proposal writing, from start to finish, is discussed in detail. The author also stresses the value of a formal needs assessment before an organization begins the grant process. Both federal and foundation grants are extensively covered. The last third of the book is devoted to a variety of appendixes. One of these is a lengthy bibliography. The others range from a sample accounting system to a list of libraries which have especially good grants resource collections.

GRANTS: HOW TO FIND OUT ABOUT THEM AND WHAT TO DO NEXT by Virginia P. White (New York: Plenum Press, 1975) is a standard reference work which is especially useful to the novice. This classic book begins by defining a grant and moves on to sources of information. Ms. White also covers foundation and government grants in some detail. She is careful to stress the groundwork necessary before an organization reaches the proposal-writing stage. She even discusses the period after the application has been filed. As with Horgen's book, the appendixes are as valuable as the text. Appendix I is especially so, being a glossary and explanation of all the different types of grants.

In a more recent book called GRANT PROPOSALS THAT SUCCEED (edited by Virginia White. New York: Plenum Press, 1983) Ms. White has compiled case histories of grants from the sciences and the humanities which are annotated and explained. The examples include both research and training grants as well as grants requesting funding for events or classes. The final section discusses the preliminary letter: both why it is important and how to write it.

Corporate Grants

Large corporations give over a billion a year to various organizations to fund a myriad of projects. These dollars tend to benefit the corporation directly or indirectly. Companies frequently provide funds for things like economic development, job training, or emergency relief in their immediate geographic area. They may also fund art or health related activities in their area. Sometimes corporations will fund projects that will benefit their market. This type of giving can be used as valuable and very positive public relations. For instance, a chain of toy stores might fund projects related to improving the welfare of children. These corporate grants need not always be money, sometimes they are gifts of equipment or services.

Most corporations run their grant programs like a business. This business-like atmosphere demands thorough preparation and standard accounting procedures on the part of the organization applying for the grant. On the other hand, corporate giving is more flexible and less bound to a set of rules and guidelines than federal or foundation giving, and so can be more responsive to emergency needs.

There are two excellent directories which cover corporate philanthropy in great detail. The first, TAFT CORPORATE GIVING DIRECTORY (edited by David E. Sharpe. 6th ed., Washington, D.C.: Taft Corp., 1985), is a collection of comprehensive profiles and analyses of the major American corporate philanthropic programs. Most of the directory is taken up by detailed program profiles. Each of these profiles gives a contact person for the program, extensive information on the types of grants and their typical recipients as well as a list of recent grants. Especially useful sections of each profile are the "who runs the company," "who runs the foundation," "who runs the contributions program," and, finally, "how to approach them."

Another source on corporate giving is CORPORATE 500: THE DIRECTORY OF CORPORATE PHILANTHROPY (5th ed., San Francisco: Public Management Institute, 1986) which reports on the 500 corporations that are most active in American philanthropy. Each corporation was researched through interviews, IRS 990 forms, published annual reports, and by direct contacts. The finished report was then sent to the corporation for verification. Some entries are incomplete because these companies refused to divulge the requested data.

The Public Management Institute recommends that their directory be used in stages. First, the indexes should be used to select a small number of companies with a high likelihood of funding the desired project. There are eleven indexes to help the researcher choose. Second, the corporation reports should be used to shape the requestor's approach. Then they recommend that the grant-seeker draw on other sources of information to polish the request.

Foundation Grants

Although some corporations do channel their philanthropic activities through foundations there are many foundations in addition to corporate ones. All of these charitable foundations give billions of dollars to organizations every year. This money is dispensed by the foundations according to their specific guidelines and procedures. They usually have relatively small staffs, which makes it difficult for them to deal with the large number of proposals that are indiscriminately submitted without regard to those guidelines. Therefore, it is to an organization's advantage to study the foundation's guidelines before undertaking the writing of grant proposals.

Nonprofit organizations interested in making a grant application should take some preliminary steps before actually filing a proposal with any foundation or agency. The first step is to become familiar with foundations and their operating procedures. There are a number of excellent books which provide good overviews of charitable foundations and their operations in addition to GRANTS by Virginia P. White and PLAYING THE FUNDING GAME by Gregory C. Horgen, which were discussed in the beginning of this chapter.

FOUNDATION FUNDAMENTALS by Patricia Read (New York: Foundation Center, 1986) is a good starting point. This book could also be subtitled "What You Should Know about Foundations before You Ask for Money." The author begins with the history of foundations and then compares foundation grants to those from other sources such as the government. FOUNDATION FUNDAMENTALS is structured to help the grant-seeker find the right foundation. Ms. Read demonstrates to the readers, first, how to organize their need and, then, how to match those needs to foundation interests.

The book is exceptionally well illustrated with many explanatory graphs, charts, and sample forms. The appendixes are also very good. They contain a section of questionnaires designed to guide the grant-seeker through the preparation period, step by step, as well as a bibliography of sources for further information on foundations. Finally, there is a section on the submission of proposals which includes a list of all the things that an organization should do before submitting a proposal.

The standard reference book for information about private foundations is THE FOUNDATION DIRECTORY (edited by Loren Renz. 10th ed., New York: The Foundation Center, 1985). The tenth edition includes entries for over 4,000 foundations. Although these foundations are only 18 percent of all those active in the United States, they account for 97 percent of the total assets and 85 percent of the money awarded. They all hold assets of at least $1 million and gave away at least $100,000 per year. Foundations are chosen for inclusion based on the IRS 990 forms that they submitted. Each one that qualifies is sent a request for information by the Foundation Center. Entries for those not responding are prepared by the Center's staff using the most recent IRS forms available. Those entries are marked in the directory with a special symbol. Foundations are listed alphabetically under the state in which they are legally established. Each entry includes a brief description of their giving interest, address, current financial data, officers, donors, and grant application procedures. There are four indexes to guide users to the entries: the name of the foundation; an alphabetical listing of all donors, trustees, and officers; geographical location; and fields of interest. THE FOUNDATION DIRECTORY is available online through DIALOG.

The Foundation Center also publishes THE FOUNDATION GRANTS INDEX (edited by Elan Goronzik and Patricia Read. 15th ed., New York: The Foundation Center, 1986) which is a cumulative listing of foundation grants. It provides access to the funding interest of major foundations by subject area, geographic focus, types of support, and the types of organizations which receive grants. These grants of $5,000 or more were awarded by approximately 100 of the United States' largest foundations as reported to The Foundation Center, and represent about half of the total grant dollars awarded.

The introduction contains a section entitled, "How to Use THE FOUN-DATION GRANTS INDEX." A thorough study of this section is recommended before attempting to use this book. Briefly the grants are by state and then alphabetically by name. Entries are indexed by foundation name, subject, and the names of the recipients. After researchers have developed a list of funding possibilities using THE FOUNDATION GRANTS INDEX they can then go to THE FOUNDATION DIRECTORY to expand and refine the list. THE FOUNDATION GRANTS INDEX is also available online through DIALOG.

Another sampling of how foundations spend their money is available in WHERE AMERICA'S LARGE FOUNDATIONS MAKE THEIR GRANTS (edited by Joseph Dermer. 5th ed., Hartsdale, N.Y.: Public Services Materials Center, 1983–84). Most of the information in this book was derived from the annual reports of the foundations and from The Foundation Center records. The foundations are arranged alphabetically by state and list the address as well as a description of that foundation's major grants. Only the total amount granted is listed for grants of $1,000. For example, the entry might read "Discretionary grants of $1,000 or less totaling $27,000."

Perhaps the most valuable field in this book is the one called "Additional Insights." Although this practically worded field is not available for each foundation, it gives straightforward, inside advice such as "Applications get quicker consideration if submitted in January, April, July, or October." In the intense competition for foundation money extra features like this can give the informed grant-seeker a great advantage.

Federal Grants

Making an application for federal grant money is quite different from applying to a foundation. There is a great deal more paper work involved and the entire process is much more structured and formal. The combination of extremely rigid rules and tighter federal money makes it harder for the novice to obtain these grants. The next two books were chosen to help beginning grant-seekers through the labyrinth of federal regulations.

One of the most important resources for federal grants is the CATALOG OF FEDERAL DOMESTIC ASSISTANCE (Washington, D.C.: Government Printing Office, 1965-   ). This looseleaf service is published annually and updated every six months. It contains information on *every* federal program that provides assistance or benefits to the American public. It is arranged by department and then by program.

The information for each program is quite detailed and an extensive series of indexes provides access to the individual program descriptions. These are indexed by agency, function, subject, applicant eligibility, and deadlines for program applications.

DEVELOPING SKILLS IN PROPOSAL WRITING by Mary Hall (2d ed., Portland, Ore.: Continuing Education Publications, 1971) is an excellent overview of the federal grants process. In the first part of the book the author takes the grant-seeker step-by-step through the pre-proposal stage, from formulating ideas to selecting a funding source. The second part is on writing the proposal and deals not only with writing the proposal but the process of evaluation, the budget, and the problems of the personnel in-volved in the project. The most common shortcomings found in rejected proposals are listed and Ms. Hall gives suggestions for overcoming them. The appendix consists of extensive checklists for every stage of the grants process, all of which should prove invaluable to the researcher.

Another useful reference on federal grants is called FEDERAL GRANTS MANAGEMENT HANDBOOK (Washington, D.C.: Grants Management Advisory Service, 1978-   ). This looseleaf service is designed as a basic reference tool for seeking federal grants. It also discusses the general re-quirements and provides the novice with authoritative and easy-to-under-stand directions. Because it is a collection of generally applicable requirements, problems will need to be addressed to a specific agency's program or administrative officials, as each agency or department has some additional requirements. This handbook also serves as an updating and monitoring service for new developments.

The Grants Management Advisory Service will also assist in identifying information or services relating to special problems for subscribers to the FEDERAL GRANTS MANAGEMENT HANDBOOK.

Conclusion

A final reference covers grants made by all three sources of funds: cor-porate, foundation, and federal. DRG: DIRECTORY OF RESEARCH GRANTS (Phoenix, Ariz.: Oryx Press, 1985) is a reference book for indi-viduals and institutions in search of support for research and other creative endeavors. It provides information which enables the researcher to directly contact the sponsoring agency. The preface to this book gives condensed, but very clear, instructions for developing a proposal and explains each part of the finished draft. The 1985 edition of the directory lists over 3,000 sources of federal, state, or private grants. DRG is available online through DIALOG as a database called GRANTS which is updated monthly.

Almost all of the information described in this chapter applies to grants made to nonprofit organizations. Most foundations do not make grants to individuals unless they are affiliated with such an organization. The Foun-dation Center's publication, FOUNDATION GRANTS TO INDIVIDUALS (edited by Loren Renz. New York: The Foundation Center, 1986), provides the individual with an alternative to affiliating with a nonprofit organization. The information in this book is compiled from Foundation Center publi-cations and IRS forms as well as other sources. It provides the most com-prehensive listing of this type available. The book is arranged according to eligibility requirements and means of access or access restriction. Each entry includes the standard information such as address, telephone number, and financial data as well as detailed information about application requirements and the nature of the award. Entries are indexed by subject, state, companies, specific educational institutions, and by foundations.

These and many other excellent books on fundraising can be found at almost any medium to large public library and at most academic libraries. Organizations thinking of requesting a grant would be well advised to study one of the basic guides mentioned earlier in this chapter and to consult a professional grants person for advice before beginning the arduous process of seeking grant money.

11

Other Media, Experts, Computer Software, and Unpublished Sources

Three of the categories discussed in this chapter all have two things in common: they are sometimes difficult to obtain and they can be some of the most valuable resources available to the researcher. There are no hard and fast rules that can be used in the search for experts, audiovisual media, or unpublished sources: there are only possible avenues of investigation. This chapter discusses some of the most important of those avenues and how they can be used to benefit the researcher. It also covers some basic sources of information on computer software.

Audiovisual Media

Nonprint media provide a valuable resource for those interested in influencing the future, especially those who are involved in the educational process. Although nonprint media are not as readily available as books and journals or online resources they are frequently much easier to obtain than is generally supposed.

The first decision that must be made is whether or not the item should be purchased. If the decision is made to purchase then the best route is the most direct one: order it from the producer or the publisher. In the event that the researcher is not interested in purchasing the production it may be rented or borrowed from a variety of sources.

Many libraries have large audiovisual collections which are available through their interlibrary loan services (See Chapter 3, Basic Facts for Beginners, for a description of interlibrary loan services). Of course these materials are available to the library's registered borrowers just as their book and periodical collections are. Catalogs for library audiovisual collections are sometimes available on request and most libraries maintain collections of these catalogs from other libraries. Many of these catalogs have subject indexes. In addition, since most libraries provide cataloging for nonprint media they can also be searched by author and title in the library's catalog.

Bibliographies of audiovisual materials for specific subject areas can usually be found. For instance, several excellent books which identify films and other audiovisual materials on influencing the future are available. In many cases short annotations are provided for each production. The most notable and the most comprehensive of these tools is THE FUTURE: A GUIDE TO INFORMATION SOURCES (2d ed., Washington, D.C.: World Future Society, 1979). THE FUTURE has chapters on films, audiotapes, games and simulations, and other media. The media are listed by subject and title and a short annotation is given for each entry along with the source for each production. The "other media" chapter deals with filmstrips and multimedia learning kits as well as slide/tape learning programs in the same way. A much broader listing of films can be found in FILMS ON THE FUTURE (Washington, D.C.: World Future Society, 1979).

In addition to the sources already discussed, many audiovisual producers publish catalogs of their offerings. These catalogs are usually available free of charge. There are also several organizations which provide information about and access to audiovisual materials.

Guides to audiovisual resources are also available for the different types of media. THE VIDEO SOURCE BOOK (7th ed., National Video Clearinghouse. Detroit: Gale Research Co., 1985) is typical of this type of source. The seventh edition provides details on over 40,000 video titles from more than 850 sources. A detailed subject index provides access to the entries which contain information such as title, availability, running time, audience rating and intended use.

EDUCATORS PROGRESS SERVICE, INC. (214 Center St., Randolph, Wis. 53956. 414/326–3126), was founded in 1934 to collect and report free material for teachers. The service has expanded and now publishes some ten guides including EDUCATORS GUIDE TO FREE FILMS (46th ed., Randolph, Wis.: Educators Progress Service, Inc., 1986) and EDUCATORS GUIDE TO FREE AUDIO AND VIDEO MATERIALS (33d ed., Randolph, Wis.: Educators Progress Service, 1986). Each guide includes annotated listings of materials arranged by title under subject headings. The guides serve only as a location tool. The user identifies the source for a film or some other type of educational material and then must go to that source to procure the material.

THE NATIONAL INFORMATION CENTER FOR EDUCATIONAL MEDIA (NICEM) (P.O. Box 40130, Albuquerque, N.M. 505/265–3591) operates a computer databank of over half a million media listings. The indexes to this massive databank are available in paperback and on microfiche. For the most part the individual indexes cover the different media formats separately although there are also several that are subject indexes to the entire collection. The most heavily used index in either book or microfiche format is the INDEX TO 16mm EDUCATIONAL FILMS (8th ed., Los Angeles: University of Southern California, 1984).

Both the paperback and the microfiche versions of NICEM publications are difficult to use. Some of the entries do not provide adequate bibliographic information and many omit important information such as the price and date. A final problem is that the source for each entry is listed in a complex code form. Fortunately for frequent users NICEM indexes are available on both BRS and DIALOG. They are especially useful in their online versions because the researcher can look in all the format and subject indexes at one time and can also limit searches by media format or grade level or any one of several available categories. Many of the entries have abstracts. This is especially true if the title is not descriptive. Also, the names and addresses of the producer and distributor are usually included.

Finally, an agency of the United States government serves as a clearinghouse for audiovisual material: the NATIONAL AUDIOVISUAL CENTER (NAC) (National Archives and Records Service, General Services Administration, Reference Section/PC, Washington, D.C. 10409. 301/763–1896). NAC was created in 1969 to provide sales and rental access for audiovisual materials produced or commissioned by federal agencies. There are approximately 13,000 programs available for rental preview, purchase, or loan in film or video formats and slide, audiotape, or multimedia kits. The last and most comprehensive listing of these materials is the REFERENCE LIST OF U.S. GOVERNMENT PRODUCED AUDIOVISUAL MATERIALS, 1978 (Washington, D.C.: U.S. Government Printing Office, 1978). The center also publishes a free, occasional newsletter called SELECTLIST which covers new materials.

A word of caution: all of these resources are merely listings. Many have no abstracts or annotations. Judgements of quality and suitability are made entirely by the person using the materials, therefore it is extremely important to allow enough time to review the production and to schedule alternative programming if necessary. Also, the more popular and timely a production, the more heavily used and the tighter its schedule: therefore, productions must be booked as far in advance as possible and schedules should remain flexible to accommodate booking difficulties. Many popular films and other media are booked months and sometimes years in advance.

Professional meetings can also provide information on audiovisual presentations. Many times these productions are being shown to members of the organization as part of the program. They are also frequently part of the exhibits which accompany the meeting. Many different companies and producers will be represented at one time as part of the exhibits and they ordinarily have free literature available. One particularly important meeting is that of the INTERNATIONAL COMMUNICATIONS INDUSTRIES AS- SOCIATION (ICIA) formerly the NATIONAL AUDIO-VISUAL ASSO- CIATION (3510 Spring St., Fairfax, Va. 22031. 703/273–7200). ICIA is a membership trade association of the communications technology industry which offers training programs in the use of all kinds of communications equipment and an annual convention with extensive exhibits as well as numerous publications. The most important of these publications is THE EQUIPMENT DIRECTORY OF AUDIO-VISUAL COMPUTER AND VIDEO PRODUCTS, 1985–86 (edited by Mary Stevens. 31st ed., Fairfax, Va.: ICIA, 1985). This comprehensive, illustrated buyer's guide has speci- fications and prices for more than 1,500 audiovisual, computer, and video products. ICIA also publishes a very useful series of brochures on choosing and using various kinds of equipment.

Computer Software

The microcomputer market has exploded within recent years. Conse- quently, software and directories of software from various markets have also proliferated wildly. There are dozens of these catalogs and directories on the market and more are being published every day. A critical review of the entire field of this literature is certainly beyond the scope of this chapter. Therefore, the following listing represents only a few of the most important and the most readily available descriptive sources for software.

There is an extremely useful directory or guidebook to "free" software called HOW TO GET FREE SOFTWARE by Alfred Glossbrenner (New York: St. Martin's Press, 1984). This book is a guide to obtaining thousands of public domain programs either free or at cost. It tells how to get word processing, communications, database management, game, educational, and other programs from user groups, bulletin board services and other places.

THE FREE SOFTWARE CATALOG AND DIRECTORY by Robert A. Froelich (New York: Crown, 1984) is a catalog of CP/M software complete with a series of indexes. Over 5,000 programs are described and indexed by key word, language, author or revisers, and title. This book also contains a list of several hundred computer bulletin boards with telephone numbers. The final section is a list of user groups with addresses. In addition, the book begins with an excellent introduction which is actually a good basic education on both CP/M and free software.

There are also several brand specific guides to free software which can be quite valuable. THE DIRECTORY OF PUBLIC DOMAIN (AND USER SUPPORTED) SOFTWARE FOR THE IBM PERSONAL COMPUTER (Santa Clara, Calif.: PC Software Interest Group, 1984) is a good example. Most local user groups maintain libraries of public domain software for the convenience of their members. In addition, some computer stores and libraries maintain similar collections.

THE SOFTWARE CATALOG (New York: Elsevier, 1986) publishes two editions, one for minicomputers and one for microcomputers. The latter is published in two volumes. Volume one contains instructions for using THE SOFTWARE CATALOG, several articles by computer experts, and approximately 1,200 pages of detailed program descriptions arranged by vendor and international standard program number. Volume two contains a series of indexes to volume one and a glossary of terms. THE SOFTWARE CATALOG is published twice a year, winter and summer and these issues are updated after three months. Entries are complete and remarkably informative even though they are brief.

Many of these sources as well as several others are discussed in an excellent article called "Common Sense and Free Software: or, If It's Free, Can It Be Any Good?" by Walt Crawford (LIBRARY HI TECH. 3(3) p. 47–56, 1985). This article reviews the field of public domain software and how to find out about it. Crawford gives an excellent description of the various operating systems and categories of free software in a series of sidebars. He also reviews several of the most popular programs. This is a personal opinion article about free software and at the same time it is an excellent overview of a very confusing area.

One of the most commonly available directories is DATASOURCES (Published quarterly: January, April, July, and October. New York: Ziff-Davis Publishing Co., 1981-   ). This quarterly publication is also divided into two volumes, hardware and software. Both contain several features in common such as product listings, company profiles, section contents page, product index, company product index, and marketline. Sections are cross-referenced to each other. For example, the product listings refer the user to the vendor's company profile. The section contents pages provide a detailed list of all the categories in that section and instructions for locating product descriptions.

The "At-a-Glance" charts are unique to the hardware volume. They provide an easy means of comparing products and are referenced to the most detailed description of each product in the product listing. The software volume's unique feature is its software package index which is an alphabetical list by package name of all the software in DATASOURCES. This index enables the user to find information about a software package even if the category or vendor for that package is not known.

One of the files unique to BRS is called SOFT or *Online Microcomputer Software Guide and Directory*. Its scope includes current product descriptions plus related information on costs, applications, purchase, hardware requirements, documentation, availability, and operating specifications as well as producer comments and critical review information on the package. SOFT contains over 1,500 records and is updated monthly, making it one of the most comprehensive sources of information about software. Its print counterpart is ONLINE MICROCOMPUTER SOFTWARE GUIDE AND DIRECTORY 1983–84 (Georgetown, Conn.: Online, Inc., 1983).

Experts

Finding experts in a specific subject area can be very difficult; however, there are a few definite places to begin research. One of the most obvious places to find expert speakers is through organizations like the INTER-NATIONAL PLATFORM ASSOCIATION (2564 Berkshire Road, Cleveland Heights, Oh. 44106. 216/932–0505). This group maintains a sort of clearinghouse for those willing to speak on certain subjects and those who are looking for a speaker.

In Chapter 7, Government Agencies and Officials, and Chapter 8, Government Documents, the discussion centered on the organization of the various governments and their publications. This same information, when viewed in another light provides some insight into identifying the specific people who are responsible for various programs. Many of these government departments have a designated person who is willing to speak and/or answer questions. Department heads and people in charge of various agencies are usually experts in their particular fields. Using the resources described in Chapter 9, Interest Groups and Networks, the researcher can identify individuals who are prominent in some group and who, presumably, are knowledgeable about the affairs of the group or network. THE ENCYCLOPEDIA OF ASSOCIATIONS, mentioned in Chapter 9, is an excellent source of experts as each association's chief executive officer is listed.

Another way of identifying experts is by word-of-mouth and by simply asking questions. This may seem obvious but many times the simplest means to an end are overlooked. Professional meetings are another rather obvious source of experts. Those who are speaking to or presiding over a meeting of their peers will certainly fall into this category.

THE FUTURES RESEARCH DIRECTORY: INDIVIDUALS (Washington, D.C.: World Future Society, 1986) updates one section of THE FUTURE: A GUIDE TO INFORMATION SOURCES which was published in 1979 and mentioned earlier in this chapter. This directory is a listing of nearly 1,000 individuals professionally involved in the study of the future. Each entry gives the person's name, addresses, telephone numbers, education, professional activities and recent publications. Specialized listings of individuals such as this or membership lists can be an important source for identifying experts. Most libraries routinely collect this kind of reference book.

Finally, experts can be identified using a simple online searching technique. By choosing an appropriate database and executing a subject search and then sorting the resulting citation by author, the researcher can identify several people with multiple articles on the subject. These names can then be researched further in some of the standard biographical resources discussed in Chapter 9, Interest Groups and Networks. This strategy is a good example of a situation information search, which is usually a combination of the various tools and techniques outlined in this book.

Unpublished Works

Finding unpublished materials is usually very difficult and time-consuming. Before beginning such a request the researcher should make every effort to locate the information in some published form. Failing that, the most direct route is to locate the author and telephone or write requesting a copy of the material.

Fortunately, some types of unpublished material such as dissertations and theses are slightly more accessible. Information about dissertations is available in print through DISSERTATION ABSTRACTS INTERNATIONAL (Ann Arbor, Mich.: University Microfilms, 1938-   ), and online through DISSERTATIONS ABSTRACTS ONLINE, file 35 on DIALOG. The former is issued monthly and has an annual cumulated index. University Microfilms can provide fiche or print copies of most of the dissertations indexed online or in print. Since 1957, each volume of the print index has a thirteenth issue which is a consolidated list of all the dissertations covered, including some which are not available through University Microfilms. DISSERTATION ABSTRACTS INTERNATIONAL is indexed by title, key word, and by author.

Another source, A GUIDE TO THESES AND DISSERTATIONS by Michael M. Reynolds (Phoenix, Ariz.: Oryx Press, 1986) is an annotated bibliography of books about theses and dissertations produced through 1985. According to the introduction each annotation is based on a personal examination of the work by Reynolds. Although they are brief, each one contains the following elements: level of the work, the number of items, the years within which the studies were completed, the institution or institutions involved, the subject coverage, the bibliographic arrangement and indexes provided. The guide itself is indexed by institution, by name and title, and by subject. As a source of sources Reynold's guide is invaluable in an area with scant bibliographic control.

Master's theses are also covered in another publication, MASTERS ABSTRACTS (Ann Arbor, Mich.: University Microfilms, 1962-   ). This publication   is   very   similar   to   DISSERTATION   ABSTRACTS INTERNATIONAL, which was discussed earlier in this chapter.

The interest groups and networks discussed in Chapter 9 can provide some access to unpublished material that is not of an academic nature. Professional meetings and their proceedings or transactions are also excellent sources of unpublished information. If the meeting is several years in the past the researcher can do an author search covering the period since the time of the meeting to determine whether or not the material has been published subsequently. Although most indexes and abstracts do not cover meeting abstracts they are indexed in the citation indexes (See Chapter 5, Abstracts and Indexes for a detailed discussion of the citation indexes) and are designated as such.

Conclusion

There are no specific guides or bibliographic sources which cover the searching out of experts and unpublished materials. These materials can be very difficult to find and are especially hard for the novice researcher. They demand all the bibliographic wiles and cunning a researcher can muster. For that reason this chapter has been placed last in the second section of INFORMATION AND THE FUTURE. This position gives the researcher the benefit of having covered all the other information sources in the book, many of which will also be valuable in locating these last two types of elusive materials.

PART III

APPLICATIONS

12

Information and Social Change

If you don't know where you want to go, you can bet you'll end up somewhere else!

—Yogi Berra

In this chapter we introduce two conceptual tools which can help you learn about, forecast, and influence the process of social change on topics of importance to you. These tools are generally quite relevant to topics as diverse as ecology or the economy, regulation or racism. If they are to be used effectively, however, they require efficient access to the information sources covered in Part II, which becomes feasible using search strategies such as those described in Part I.

Because it would take far more words to *verbally* describe how to use these tools than is feasible here, this chapter relies heavily on *graphical* illustrations to convey a practical understanding of the tools. Moreover, we do not, in general, explain each and every facet of these graphical illustrations. Instead we assume that readers will envision for themselves how the process being depicted can be applied to their own needs. Readers finding it difficult to understand how to implement these concepts may therefore want to consult the references cited in connection with each for additional help. It may also be helpful to read the case study presented in Chapter 13 before proceeding, since it depicts a concrete situation in which these tools can be used. Finally, we would point out that, complicated as these tools may seem to persons new to the study of social change and change management, they represent a considerable simplification of the complexity of the numerous approaches which they synthesize.

The Issue Emergence Cycle

About ten years ago, one of the pioneers of the modern futures research movement, Graham T. T. Molitor, discovered that potentially important issues emerge gradually in society. Furthermore, issues often appear in different types of media at different phases of their development. Significantly, most public policy issues appeared to follow a similar pattern of development, which led to the notion of an "issue emergence cycle."

Illustration 12.1 portrays an idealized version of the process which Molitor discovered. It depicts a definite sequence of stages through which a public policy issue comes into being, develops and is resolved—with the amount of public attention on the issue tending to increase as the issue emerges, peaking when a new policy is enacted or some other type of event resolves the issue for the time being.

Illustration 12.2 provides an equally idealized summary of this sequence, but from an information researcher's point of view. It depicts how different types of awareness and different types of media tend to predominate at specific stages. The arrows between popular and government awareness are meant to indicate only that either can precede the other, depending on the dynamics surrounding the specific issue.

Finally, Illustration 12.3, by detailing these properties even further, provides a cartographic checklist which the information researcher can use to more efficiently gauge the current status of a given issue. It begins with reports of early awareness of the issue, followed by conjectures and research studies as to causes, effects, and implications of the various aspects of the issue. As knowledge and information slowly accumulate, unsubstantiated "prophecies" gradually become substantiated, at least in the public's mind. As the issue continues to evolve, political positions and action-oriented agenda regarding the issue are collaboratively developed by opinion leaders in various parts of society, and are reported by the media which are most associated with each. Propagandizing and "pseudo-events" (events staged specifically in order to promulgate a particular point of view in the mass media) often become a significant part of the information environment through which public debate on the issue is reported. Resolution of the issue, whether through passage of new laws, regulations, or other mechanisms, usually leads to a marked decrease in the amount of media coverage, and the issue tends to be covered by retrospective analyses and interpretations.

Two important uses to which the Issue Emergence Cycle concept can be put are:

Illustration 12.1
Life Cycle of a Strategic Issue

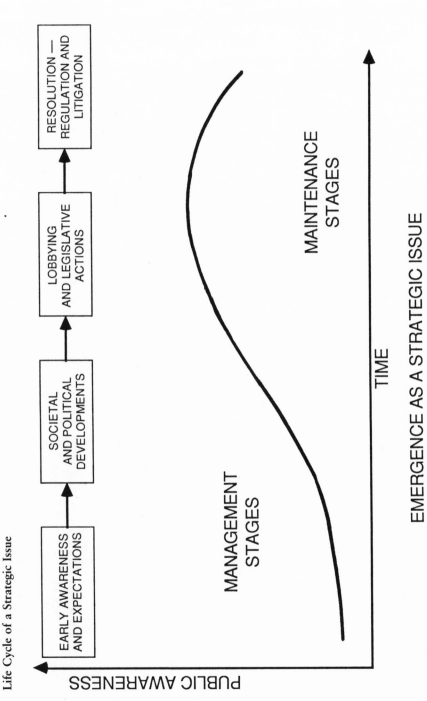

EARLY AWARENESS AND EXPECTATIONS

SOCIETAL AND POLITICAL DEVELOPMENTS

LOBBYING AND LEGISLATIVE ACTIONS

RESOLUTION — REGULATION AND LITIGATION

PUBLIC AWARENESS

MANAGEMENT STAGES

MAINTENANCE STAGES

TIME

EMERGENCE AS A STRATEGIC ISSUE

Illustration 12.2
Precursor Monitoring of Emerging Issues

IDEA CREATION	ELITE AWARENESS	POPULAR AWARENESS	GOVERNMENT AWARENESS	ENACTMENT OF NEW POLICY
MONOGRAPHS, SPECIALIZED PERIODICALS, SCIENCE FICTION	TRADE JOURNALS, RESEARCH REPORTS, NEWSLETTERS, AND "DOPESHEETS"	NEWS PERIODICALS	LEGISLATIVE HEARINGS AND ANALYSIS	LEGISLATIVE RECORD, FEDERAL REGISTER, NEWSLETTERS

MEDIA COVERAGE AND PUBLIC AWARENESS

Illustration 12.3
Communicating about Emerging Issues

VISIONARY UNINHIBITED	• ARTISTIC, POETIC WORKS • SCIENCE FICTION
RENDERING IDEA TO SPECIFICS	• FRINGE MEDIA, UNDERGROUND PRESS • UNPUBLISHED NOTES AND SPEECHES • MONOGRAPHS, TREATISES
ELABORATION OF DETAILS	• SCIENTIFIC, TECHNICAL, PROFESSIONAL JOURNALS • HIGHLY SPECIALIZED, NARROW-VIEWPOINT JOURNALS • STATISTICAL DOCUMENTS (SOCIAL INDICATORS, STATISTICAL SERVICES) • ABSTRACTING SERVICES, JOURNALS
DIFFUSION OF AN IDEA AMONG OPINION LEADERS	• DATASEARCH COMPOSITES • EGGHEAD JOURNALS (e.g., SCIENCE, SCIENTIFIC AMERICAN) • INSIDER "DOPESHEETS" (e.g., PRODUCT SAFETY LETTER)
INSTITUTIONAL RESPONSE	• POPULAR INTELLECTUAL MAGAZINES (e.g., HARPERS) • NETWORK COMMUNICATIONS (BULLETINS, NEWSLETTERS) • JOURNALS FOR THE CAUSE (e.g., CONSUMER REPORTS)
MASS MEDIA	• GENERAL INTEREST PUBLICATIONS (e.g., TIME, NEWSWEEK) • CONDENSTION OF GENERAL LITERATURE (e.g., READER'S DIGEST)
POLITICIZING THE ISSUE	• POLL DATA, PUBLIC OPINION, BEHAVIORAL AND VOTER ATTITUDES • LEGISLATIVE, GOVERNMENTAL SERVICES, REPORTS • BOOKS :
INSTANTANEOUS COVERAGE FOR MASS CONSUMPTION	• FICTION -- NOVELS PROVIDE SOCIAL ANALYSIS OF THE TIMES • NON-FICTION -- PULL TOGETHER DISCORDANT PARTS INTO EASILY UNDERSTOOD WHOLE • NEWSPAPERS (NEW YORK TIMES & WASHINGTON POST EARLY, SOUTHERN RURAL PAPERS LATE COMMENTATORS • RADIO & TELEVISION (NETWORKS COMMENT EARLIER THAN LOCAL STATIONS)
EDUCATING THE PEOPLE TO THE NEW NORM	• EDUCATION JOURNALS • HISTORICAL ANALYSES
HISTORICAL ANALYSIS	• TRADITIONAL DOCTORAL THESES

1. To help guide the process of "environmental *scanning*" for new ideas, emerging trends or significant events which would strongly affect aspects of the future about which you are most concerned; and when identified, to *monitor* their progress across time. This provides an improved sense of both the social change process through which issues of concern are defined and influenced, and of the immediate status of any specific issue of concern.

2. To better estimate when differing social change strategies may work most effectively; and in particular, when to use specific types of media in order to best communicate your point of view in order to get your message across to the audience that is important at that stage.

Although Molitor has written a number of different items on the Issue Emergence Cycle for various clients of his firm, Public Policy Forecasting,

Inc., most of them are unpublished. Similar ideas, however, have been published by Hazel Henderson in HOW TO COPE WITH ORGANIZATIONAL FUTURE SHOCK (Management Review, pp. 19–28, July 1976) and in CREATING ALTERNATIVE FUTURES (New York: Berkley, 1978). Probably the most concise published information on the use of this conceptual tool is to be found in ISSUES MANAGEMENT: HOW YOU CAN PLAN, ORGANIZE, AND MANAGE FOR THE FUTURE by J. Coates, V. Coates, J. Jarrat and L. Heinz (Mt. Airy, Md.: Lomond Publications, 1986). A brief publication which describes how the Molitor insight and two related models were useful in understanding the emergence of two public policy issue problems is MODELS FOR ISSUES MANAGEMENT: SUPERFUND AND RCRA AS TEST CASES by L. Heinz and J. Coates (Prepared for the Environmental Emerging Issues Team, Edison Electric Institute, 1111 19th St. N.W., Washington, D.C. 20036, 1986).

The Strategic Intelligence Cycle

In addition to having a sense of how public policy issues emerge in the body politic, it is also important to accurately envision:

- the nature of important cause and effect relationships and cross-cutting factors which influence the issue strongly;
- how the issue and related factors are perceived by important interest groups; and
- the workings of different social institutions and systems in which the issue is embedded.

Moreover, if you wish to be *proactive* rather than *reactive*, creatively responding to future conditions rather than just reacting to things as they take their course, your inquiry needs to include an exploration of possible, probable, and preferable future states of the issue as well. All told, it is a demanding task!

A second conceptual tool, the Strategic Intelligence Cycle represents a practical method of approach through which these difficult understandings can be developed within realistic time and resource constraints. It is a future-oriented synthesis of the methods and styles that good lobbyists, regional development leaders, and other successful social change agents tend to use in their day-to-day work.

Overview of the Model

A skeletal overview of the Strategic Intelligence Cycle is presented in Illustration 12.4. Note that in addition to helping select preferred strategies for directly influencing change, the Cycle also emphasizes the *refinement* of information seeking—*once it is clear what action-oriented strategies the*

Illustration 12.4
An Overview of the Strategic Intelligence Cycle

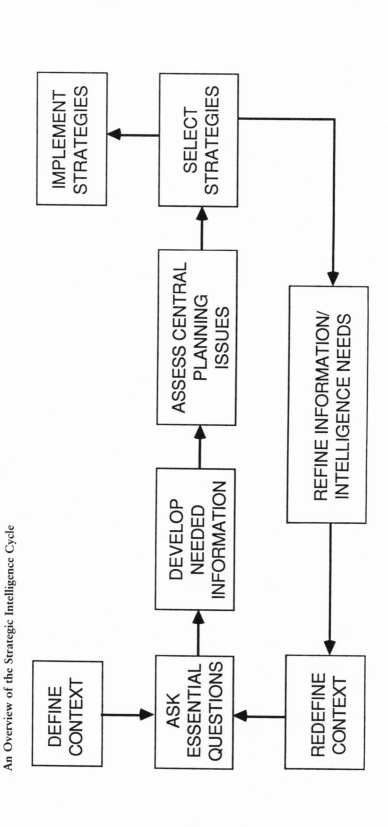

Illustration 12.5
The Strategic Intelligence Cycle

Phase 1: Get Underway

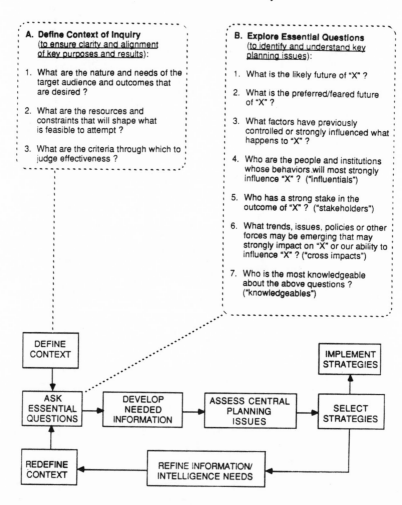

A. Define Context of Inquiry
(to ensure clarity and alignment
of key purposes and results):

1. What are the nature and needs of the
   target audience and outcomes that
   are desired ?

2. What are the resources and
   constraints that will shape what
   is feasible to attempt ?

3. What are the criteria through which to
   judge effectiveness ?

B. Explore Essential Questions
(to identify and understand key
planning issues):

1. What is the likely future of "X" ?

2. What is the preferred/feared future
   of "X" ?

3. What factors have previously
   controlled or strongly influenced what
   happens to "X" ?

4. Who are the people and institutions
   whose behaviors will most strongly
   influence "X" ? ("influentials")

5. Who has a strong stake in the
   outcome of "X" ? ("stakeholders")

6. What trends, issues, policies or other
   forces may be emerging that may
   strongly impact on "X" or our ability to
   influence "X" ? ("cross impacts")

7. Who is the most knowledgeable
   about the above questions ?
   ("knowledgeables")

DEFINE
CONTEXT

IMPLEMENT
STRATEGIES

ASK
ESSENTIAL
QUESTIONS

DEVELOP
NEEDED
INFORMATION

ASSESS CENTRAL
PLANNING
ISSUES

SELECT
STRATEGIES

REDEFINE
CONTEXT

REFINE INFORMATION/
INTELLIGENCE NEEDS

information is intended to support. Toward this end, the "80–20 rule" and
other advice offered in Chapter 2 in connection with the "Information
Wheel" is of *vital* importance. After reading this chapter in its entirety,
readers may find it useful to review Chapter 2 before attempting to adapt
and apply this conceptual model to their needs.

Sequenced Exposition of the Model

The first phase of the process, *Get Underway,* is detailed on Illustration
12.5. A variety of checklists exist through which to ensure that there is good

Illustration 12.6
Important Contextual Factors

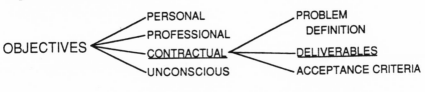

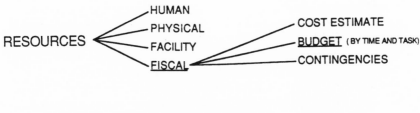

alignment between the purposes, the resources, constraints, and criteria for judging successful outcomes (all of which are considered in the first step, Definition of Context), before beginning. One such list is the Guided Design Process introduced in Chapter 1 and portrayed there as Illustration 1.3. The importance of the contextual checklist shown in Illustration 12.6 is difficult to overstate. The six items which it underscores are, in many situations, what get you in trouble if they haven't been carefully defined from the outset.

The second step of getting underway, *Explore Essential Questions*, is similar to the "five W's" (Who, What, When, Where, Why) asked by investigative reporters; but here we are dealing more with the future than the past. In order to make the method of approach as general as possible, we use the symbol "X" to refer to whatever issue is of interest to you. (Note, however that although only a single "X" is explicitly mentioned in the Strategic Intelligence Cycle, you will usually have to work simultaneously with numerous factors or issues—not a single "X"—in most practical applications of the method. In the scenario presented in Chapter 13 as a case study, for example, "X" initially refers to "regional well-being in Mid City," but the focus expands quickly to include various other factors involved in regional well-being: sustainable economic development and quality of life;

with quality of life being in turn subdivided into water quality, water availability, traffic congestion and so-forth. (Obviously it helps to have some clear way of keeping track of what you are working on at any point in time, and how it affects related issues of interest.)

The second major phase of the approach, *Develop a Change-Oriented Information Framework* (Illustration 12.7), provides not only a way to keep track of the different issues you are working on, but also to see how these issues are changing across time, and on other viewpoints important to stay abreast of when engaging in collaborative efforts to influence a given issue.

The third phase, *Assess Central Planning Issues* (Illustration 12.8), is deceptively simple in appearance and complex to implement successfully, but people who care about effective change management find a way to cover all of the questions which it addresses. In approaching these questions for the first time, readers may find the simpler checklist of questions presented in Chapter 1 (Illustration 1.4) a useful way to begin.

In Illustration 12.9, we present the fourth phase, *Select Strategies*, together with the fifth, *Refine Information/Intelligence Needs*, in order to highlight the fact that in a rapidly changing society, it is frequently necessary to have up-to-date information on the types of factors described above in order to successfully implement whatever strategies you choose; and therefore, your continuing research and analysis needs to be refined so as to support the newly chosen strategy or strategies in as direct a manner as possible. Otherwise your information gathering will tend to be merely academic. The case study presented in the next chapter illustrates several such "mid-course corrections."

Methods for Strategic Development and Change Management

Summary Comments about the Two Conceptual Models

Experienced practitioners will recognize that the above depiction of the Issue Emergence Cycle and the Strategic Intelligence Cycle, although moderately detailed, represents a vast simplification of matters that are highly complex and often ambiguous. They were presented, not with the idea that they will rigorously mirror all situations that you are likely to encounter when using them, but with the knowledge that, when combined with the search methods presented in Chapter 2, it should be feasible for you to *learn* whatever you need to *adapt* them successfully. Together, they offer an approach through which to ethically grasp and to influence the social change processes in the industrialized democracies of the world, in spite of the fact that these processes are too complex, too ambiguous, and too rapidly changing to be described in a single book or set of books. They are methods for shared foresight and proactive management—what has sometimes been called "anticipatory democracy."

Illustration 12.7
The Strategic Intelligence Cycle

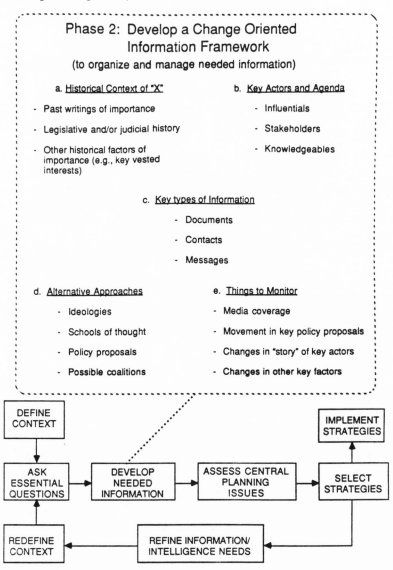

The organizational capacity to use these methods, however, doesn't just happen—it must be created. Although they admittedly go beyond that which is conventionally believed feasible to practice in most real world organizations, we next introduce four sets of methods which comprise the state-of-the-art for making it practical and effective.

Illustration 12.8
The Strategic Intelligence Cycle

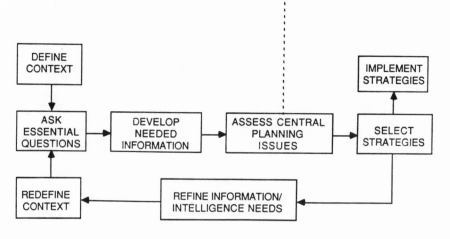

PHASE 3. Assess Central Planning Issues
(to develop appropriate strategies)

a. <u>Identify critical factors, obstacles and incentives</u>

What factors must be influenced if the future of "X" is to become what we want it to be ?

What obstacles are likely to prevent us from influencing things as we would like ?

What incentives can be brought to bear to overcome obstacles ?

b. <u>Estimate critical timing relationships</u>

Are any key factors likely to become "acute" and require a crisis-reaction strategy that would be less effective or more costly than a proactive response ?

What is the likely sequence and timing of events that will most strongly influence "X" assuming that we do not intervene "proactively" ?

c. <u>Identify Probable and Desirable Roles</u>

Who are the relevant players ?

What is the range of roles that each is likely to play, assuming either that we do, or that we do not act proactively ?

DEFINE CONTEXT				IMPLEMENT STRATEGIES
ASK ESSENTIAL QUESTIONS	DEVELOP NEEDED INFORMATION	ASSESS CENTRAL PLANNING ISSUES		SELECT STRATEGIES
REDEFINE CONTEXT	REFINE INFORMATION/ INTELLIGENCE NEEDS			

Methodologies for Strategic Development

Illustration 12.10 lists a set of key approaches through which to develop and use the organizational capacity for strategically navigating environmental "sea states" involving great environmental turbulence and uncer-

Illustration 12.9
The Strategic Intelligence Cycle

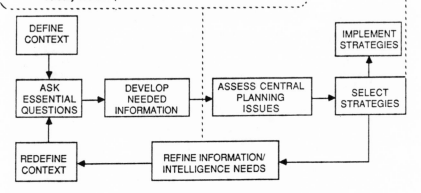

Phase 4.   Select Strategies
(to successfully influence the future of "X")

- Take direct action

- Engage in single-issue lobbying

- Collaborate with coalition networks to develop a broad range of proactive agenda

- Publicize selected issues or points of view

- Develop needed information to answer critical questions

**Phase 5.   Refine Information/
            Intelligence Needs**

a. Type of Information

- Statistical data

- Authoritative reports

- Knowledgeable experts

b. Immediacy of Source

- Primary sources (personal communication or original writing)

- Secondary Sources (popular literature, news media, trade/professional working papers, etc.

- Tertiary sources (summaries, abstracts, indexes, etc.)

tainty. Although they are often used independently, they work better when integrated within an appropriate organizational framework.

Before reading on, readers may find it useful to study Illustration 12.10 long enough to visualize for themselves how the four groups of approaches

Illustration 12.10
Methodologies for Strategic Development

1. **Issues, Intelligence, and Assessment**
   (the identification and assessment of critical planning
   issues likely to have make or break significance for the
   organizational mission)

   . Environmental scanning
   . Identification of key strengths, weaknesses,
     opportunities and threats
   . Issues management
   . Other methodologies
     (e.g., risk assessment, lobbying, public relations)

2. **Strategic Forecasting and Scenario Development**
   (the analysis and visualization of current trends, emerging
   events, and other forces for change, and how they comprise
   distinct <u>environmental contexts</u> which must be planned for)

   . Predictive forecasting
   . Contingency forecasting
   . Alternative future scenarios
   . Other methodologies
     (e.g., technology/environmental impact assessment)

3. **Strategic Planning and Policy Development**
   (the development and/or updating of mission, objectives,
   strategic policies, tactical resources, and operational
   programs needed to realize the organization's mission--even
   in face of unpredictable changes in the environment)

   . Operational planning
   . Long-range planning
   . Contingency planning
   . Planning of planning
   . Other methodologies
     (e.g., "back of the envelope" thinking,
     "networking," and "muddling through"

4. **Human and Organization Development**
   (the fostering of a valid sense of vision regarding new
   priorities, and the facilitation of human and organizational
   realignment, creative renewal, planned change and other
   outcomes necessary to achieve them)

   . Re-visioning, team building, training and
     human resource development
   . Organizational assessment, survey feedback
     and organization renewal
   . Other methodologies
     (e.g., quality circles)

might fit in organizations that they are familiar with. Additionally, it would
be useful to think about the relationship between these approaches and
those described earlier in this chapter. For more information on how to
implement these four groupings of approaches the following sources may
be consulted.

Issues, Intelligence, and Assessment

A recent and very usable book is ISSUES MANAGEMENT: HOW YOU CAN PLAN, ORGANIZE, AND MANAGE FOR THE FUTURE by J. F. Coates, V. T. Coates, J. Jarrat, and L. Heinz (Mt. Airy, Md.: Lomond Publications, 1986). An older, but much more comprehensive book is A GUIDEBOOK FOR TECHNOLOGY ASSESSMENT AND IMPACT ANALYSIS by Porter, et al. (New York: North Holland, 1980.) A nation-wide system for using these tools is described in THE STATE SCANNING NETWORK: AN ISSUE IDENTIFICATION SYSTEM FOR STATE POL-ICY MANAGERS by Lauren Cook (*Futures Research Quarterly*. Vol. 2, no. 1, Spring 1986, pp. 65–77).

Strategic Forecasting and Scenario Development

Before citing various "how to" books in this category, it is important to introduce the major conclusion of FORECASTING: AN APPRAISAL FOR POLICY-MAKERS AND PLANNERS by W. Ascher (Baltimore: The Johns-Hopkins University Press, 1978). This book analyzes the historical accuracy of predictive forecasting in a variety of important fields, and concludes that accuracy is less a function of using a sophisticated forecasting methodology than of having an accurate sense of what is going on. In other words, the accuracy of the forecaster's assumptions about major cause and effect re-lationships (which in the Strategic Intelligence Cycle we called "factors") that influence the variable being forecast is more essential to good forecasting than having the "right" methodology. Among other things, this means that it is often better to find the information you need to make your own judg-ments about future possibilities than to trust forecasts based on seemingly rigorous methods—and the "essential questions" listed in Illustration 12.5 is an excellent checklist to help you discover the categories of information likely to prove useful for this purpose.

That having been said, it is also important to distinguish between *pre-dictive* forecasting and the exploration/projection of strategically created *alternative* future scenarios (which may range from possible to probable to desirable/undesirable). Books on forecasting also differ as to whether they are written more for technical readers ("professionals") interested in fore-casting as a tool to improve the management of organizations or more action-oriented readers ("concerned citizens") interested in forecasting as a way to inform the setting of proactive political agenda.

Good books dealing with predictive forecasting from a technical per-spective are: THE HANDBOOK OF FORECASTING: A MANAGER'S GUIDE by S. Makradakis and S. Wheelwright (New York: Wiley, 1987), LONG-RANGE FORECASTING: FROM CRYSTAL BALL TO COM-PUTER by J. Armstrong (New York: Wiley, 2d ed., 1985). Among books

dealing with the broader topic of alternative future scenarios, for reasons
of both brevity and practical relevance we recommend: PLANNING UN-
DER UNCERTAINTY: MULTIPLE SCENARIOS AND CONTINGENCY
PLANNING by R. O'Conner (New York: The Conference Board, Report
No. 741, 1978); and the two-part article, SCENARIOS: UNCHARTED
WATERS AHEAD and SCENARIOS: SHOOTING THE RAPIDS by P.
Wack (*Harvard Business Review*, September/October 1985, pp. 73–89, and
November/December 1985, pp. 139–150). A somewhat longer and broader
coverage is to be found in LOOKING FORWARD: A GUIDE TO FUTURES
RESEARCH by O. Helmer (Beverly Hills, Calif.: Sage, 1983).

Probably the best introduction to alternative futures thinking as it applies
to the management of social change is SEVEN TOMORROWS: TOWARD
A VOLUNTARY HISTORY by P. Hawkin, J. Ogilvy and P. Schwartz (New
York: New American Library, 1982). It is an extremely readable paperback
that provides a useful context for all of Part III of this handbook as well
as the other readings in this section.

Strategic Planning and Policy Development

Although the phrase "strategic management" has, in some circles, su-
perceded both policy development and strategic planning by incorporating
them into a single process, there is merit in considering them separately.
One good reason is that good texts exist on both phases. Of the many useful
works on these general topics, we recommend the following due to the way
they complement each other in covering the entire topic: PUTTING IT ALL
TOGETHER: A GUIDE TO STRATEGIC THINKING by W. Rothschild
(New York: American Management Association, 1976); STRATEGIC
PLANNING: WHAT EVERY MANAGER MUST KNOW by G. Steiner
(New York: The Free Press, 1979); The O'Conner Report, PLANNING
UNDER UNCERTAINTY: MULTIPLE SCENARIOS AND CONTIN-
GENCY PLANNING, cited in the preceding section; STRATEGIES FOR
POLICY MAKING by G. Starling (Chicago: Dorsey, 1988); THE POLITICS
OF POLICY IMPLEMENTATION by R. Nakamura and I. Smallwood
(New York: St. Martin's Press, 1980). Finally, we recommend STRATEGIC
MANAGEMENT by R. McGlashan and T. Singleton (Columbus: Merrill,
1987) as a good academic text for business applications; and for public
sector applications we recommend STRATEGIC MANAGEMENT AND
UNITED WAY—A GUIDELINE SERIES (Alexandria, Va.: Strategic Plan-
ning Division, United Way of America, 1987) which includes: 1. STRA-
TEGIC MANAGEMENT AND UNITED WAY; 2. ENVIRONMENTAL
ANALYSIS; 3. ORGANIZATIONAL ASSESSMENT; 4. STRATEGIC DI-
RECTION; 5. STRATEGIC PLAN; 6. IMPLEMENTATION; 7. PERFOR-
MANCE EVALUATION; AND 8. CASE STUDIES. As part of the same
effort that produced the above materials, the United Way of America also

has produced WHAT LIES AHEAD—A MID-DECADE VIEW: AN EN-VIRONMENTAL SCAN REPORT (1985) that should be quite useful to many readers. In the next chapter, we illustrate one of many possible applications through which these tools can be put to use.

13

The Future of Economic
Development and Quality of Life
in Mid City: A Scenario

The following scenario is presented to illustrate how the methods and tools described in preceding chapters can be combined in a complex, real-world setting. The particular situation we have chosen for this purpose reflects a growing concern of many people today: the promotion of regional well-being.

The scenario is fictional, both to make it more general and to avoid the political sensitivity of describing an actual community. It is, however, based on the experiences of a number of different regions of the United States. Although fictional, the scenario is realistic in that it shows how political considerations must often shape the research process if future-oriented information and intelligence is to be accepted and used by those for whom it is intended, and thereby support the creation of shared foresight and collaborative, proactive leadership—both within and across the major institutions of society. The scenario is also somewhat unrealistic, deliberately so, in that it vastly overplays the role which information research *usually* plays in regional management. To improve this situation is, of course, part of the purpose of this chapter.

"Before Beginning"

Like many political stories, this scenario has two beginnings: an official and an unofficial one. The unofficial story begins with three socially conscious professionals talking at a party about the future of the city and surrounding region in which they live. (For convenience, the identity of both

the city and the region will be combined under the single title "Mid City".)
Being concerned that significant long-range problems and opportunities in
Mid City were apparently being ignored, they decided to spend an evening
a week studying the situation, gathering whatever information they could,
with the aim of communicating what they found to selected leaders in the
area—people of influence who might be willing to act on whatever the three
might come up with. They knew that if their investigation was done in a
relevant, but non-threatening, way, they might be able to excite the interest
of community leaders in Mid City. Many of these leaders were already quite
concerned—both about increasingly widespread unemployment in the region, and about a long-term trend that was not often talked about in public
forums, the declining base of agricultural and industrial employment in the
region and its lack of new directions of growth—a trend which if not
reversed, would spell long-term economic difficulties for Mid City.

The skills and orientations represented in the group of three, a business
professional, a teacher/graduate student, and a volunteer political activist
are significant, due to the way in which they complemented each other both
as individuals, and as representatives of three key societal institutions (the
business community, academia, and the civic sector). Relevant characteristics of each were as follows.

The first was a planning analyst from a local corporation involved in real
estate development. She, like others on the Board of Directors of the Mid
City Chamber of Commerce in which she was active, had a strongly vested
interest in the continued economic vitality of the region. Due to her contacts
there and among regional leaders generally, she usually "fronted" for the
group.

The second was a both a teacher of gifted high school students and herself
a graduate student. Having recently completed a course on "information
age tools and how to use them" in which she learned about the various
types of information sources and tools described in this handbook, she had
begun teaching her gifted high school students how to do custom-designed
information searching, and was now looking for a "real-world" application
where these newly learned skills could be put to use. She was especially
looking for a situation in which information research could be used to help
different organizations to collaborate in influencing the future of the region
for everyone's mutual benefit.

The third member of the group was a frequent lobbyist for the League
of Women Voters. Although familiar with the influence processes used in
local, regional, state and national politics, she had never been involved in
non-partisan "lobbying for the future," and was quite excited about this
possibility as a new type of outlet through which the League could help
strengthen the democratic process.

(Although the three individuals described here are meant to be broadly
representative of the body politic, we have chosen the editorial device of

writing "she" as a symbolic way of signalling the participation of both women and minorities in the activity. Similarly, although the scenario is, for convenience, written around the efforts of *three* individuals with well-defined characteristics, it is equally realistic to think of a committee of six or more, each of whom have some of these characteristics, or of a single individual who combines most of them into one complex set of roles.)

The first task of the group was to think through most of the questions posed by the Strategic Intelligence Cycle introduced in Chapter 12, which they did using the simplified "80/20–back of the envelope" type of approach which is described in Chapter 2 of this handbook. In doing this, they naturally used many of the same search processes described later in this chapter, but in an informal, exploratory way.

What they learned as a result of their brief investigation, particularly about approaches that had worked well in other regions of the country, led them to informally lobby selected leaders in the Mid City region with the idea of a blue ribbon task force on the future made up of leaders from all major interest groups in the region—a Commission to get the ball rolling. Knowing that Mid City's leaders were usually reluctant to talk publicly about regional problems due to the political risks involved in so doing, the group was somewhat surprised at how powerful the informal, but solid research base and political network they were developing worked as a base from which to argue that tangible, politically expedient steps could be taken to consider both short and long-range concerns.

"After Beginning"

So it was that the *Mid City Economic Development Commission* (MCEDC)—an ad hoc task force representing all major interest groups in the region—was created. At a press conference announcing the formation of the Commission, the Mayor and the Director of the Chamber of Commerce each called attention to the promise of high technology and economic diversification for the creation of new jobs. The president of a local college, on the other hand, emphasized the need to attract or create a "high tech infrastructure" that would include a highly skilled labor pool with the capacity for advanced R&D and state-of-the-art job retraining as well as for the other types of services that support manufacturing and service—if the "high tech" vision for the region was to be realized. No one at the press conference mentioned either alternatives to "high tech" as a way to achieve economic diversification, or "quality of life" issues as being of significant concern.

The MCEDC Strategic Development Subcommittee

Although the MCEDC engaged in a number of activities, we focus here only on those undertaken by a subcommittee which was to report to the

MCEDC Executive Director and Steering Committee, and given the responsibility for what was called:

strategic development—research and technical assistance leading to information,
intelligence, and improved ways to implement recommended action items.

The first charge to the Strategic Development Subcommittee (which was
spear-headed by the same three persons described above), was a short-term
one: *to determine what are the factors which are needed in order to attract
and maintain a healthy "high tech" infrastructure in the region.*

A second, and much longer-term outlook was also to be explored as time
permitted: *to describe the strategic context of Mid City* (regional, national,
planetary), *identifying other key planning issues that should also be considered by the MCEDC.* (Although most of the Steering Committee had
little or no feeling for what this might involve, they accepted the advice of
the Strategic Development Committee that such an inquiry was also
needed—if only to detect global trends that might otherwise take them by
surprise as had the oil embargo of 1973.)

A synopsis of the entire series of inquiries that the subcommittee reported
out to the steering committee (and later to the entire Commission) is displayed in Illustration 13.1. Readers wishing to get a quick feel for the logical
flow from start to finish may wish to study it somewhat carefully before
reading further.

Illustrative Intelligence for Sustainable Development

The following searches, although not always done in the order in which
they are described, were reported out in the following sequence to the Mid
City Economic Development Commission.

Search One: High Technology Siting Factors

Because one of the first decisions made by the MCEDC was to attract
and encourage more high technology work in the region, a first formal
information search to be done by the subcommittee was to identify the
major factors that business corporations, particularly high technology ones,
typically consider in the selection of one region over another as a site for
operations.

This turned out to be a "precision search" that was quite easy to accomplish online, using one of the commercially available computerized databases
described in Chapter Six of the handbook. Although not displayed here,
this search began with the same type of "DIALINDEX" search as was
illustrated in Chapter 1 for locating the best of many available databanks
covering this topic. As Illustration 13.2 shows, a search for writings focusing

Illustration 13.1
Illustrative Searches Undertaken by the Mid City Strategic Development Subcommittee

SEARCH TITLE	FOCUS OF SEARCH	SUMMARIZED FINDING
1. High Tech Siting Factors	Want to know how to develop "information age" sources of employment in the region: What are the criteria needing to be fulfilled in order to attract and keep a healthy "high tech" infrastructure in a given region ?	Collaborative strategies for maintaining quality of life and related factors are important but often overlooked.
2. Regional Planning Issues	Want to know what planning issues must be given priority to ensure regional well-being: What are the specific factors which MidCity needs to focus on in order to promote both economic development and quality of life satisfactorily ?	Transportation, water, and lack of collaboration among various interests in the region are major concerns.
3. Interest Groups by Planning Issue	Want to know who is a "party at interest" regarding key planning issues and may want to collaboratively influence outcomes: What specific individuals or groups already have, or might wish to actively influence the future of transportation, water, or proactive collaboration in Mid City ?	Much pentup concern exists about these issues, but no one sees a practical way to overcome short-term "turf-territoriality" oriented agenda of competing groups in the region.
4. Interest Groups by Power and Position	Want to know which of these stakeholders has taken a defined stand and amassed significant political power towards that end: What is the relative power of specific groups and "influentials" that have positions on the three planning issues ?	Although no influentials have yet championed long-range agenda on the three planning issues, a "critical mass" looks possible if the MCEDC took a strong lead.
5. Exemplary Mechanisms and Practices for Regional Development	Want to know what has worked well in other regions having similar problems: What specific mechanisms and practices have worked effectively elsewhere, and what did it take to implement them successfully ?	An omnibus public-private umbrella organization with well-articulated initiatives to meet key needs can improve things significantly.
6. Strategic Outlook for Regional Development	Want to know the general future of the region, nation, and planet in order to think about planning and management more effectively: What major trends, trend reversals, emerging issues and implications for leaders are currently important ?	Rapidly changing employment base, unpredictable economic fluctuations and increasing international competition make collaborative regional development essential.

only on site selection for high technology firms yielded forty-five "hits." A quick online scan of abstracts for the first ten or so indicated that *quality of life* was a central factor in most of them. It was therefore used to further delimit the search, bringing the total to twenty-four several of which are displayed in Illustration 13.3.

The published information turned up by this brief search on site selection indicated that two types of issues clearly stand out as "first tier" criteria in most high technology site selection decisions:

1. *Business infrastructure* considerations, including availability of water and other basic resources, appropriate buildings and transportation; favorable business climate—low taxes, loan availability, and so forth; and

Illustration 13.2
Online Search for Factors Influencing High Technology Site Selection

```
File  15:ABI/Inform - 71-87/Aug, Week 3
(Copr. UMI/Data Courier  1987)

       Set  Items  Description
       ---  -----  -----------
?ss site?(f)select?

       S1    6297  SITE?
       S2   29495  SELECT?
       S3    1578  SITE?(F)SELECT?
?s hitech? or high(w)tech? or advanced(w)tech?

               4  HITECH?
           44495  HIGH
           70221  TECH?
            3968  HIGH(W)TECH?
            5642  ADVANCED
           70221  TECH?
             596  ADVANCED(W)TECH?
       S4    4496  HITECH? OR HIGH(W)TECH? OR ADVANCED(W)TECH?
?s s4 or hi(w)tech?

            4496  S4
             171  HI
           70221  TECH?
              49  HI(W)TECH?
       S5    4516  S4 OR HI(W)TECH?
?s s3 and s5

            1578  S3
            4516  S5
       S6      45  S3 AND S5

t6/5/1-10

s s3 and quality(1w)life

            1578  S3
           23340  QUALITY
           21037  LIFE
             657  QUALITY(1W)LIFE
       S7      24  S3 AND QUALITY(1W)LIFE
?t7/5/1-24
```

Illustration 13.3
Illustrative Findings from Search One on Site Selection

7/7/1
86034539
  Location Choice in Not-for-Profit Corporations
  Erenburg, Mark; Schuldt, Richard
  Economic Development Review v4n2 PP: 16-23 Summer 1986
  AVAILABILITY: ABI/INFORM

   Factors in not-for-profit association location decision making were
identified. In January and February of 1985, survey instruments were mailed
to 485 not-for-profit organizations; 139 surveys were completed. Included
were descriptive questions plus ratings of the importance of these 7 site
attributes: 1. facilities, 2. employees, 3. support services, 4.
transportation, 5. costs of living, 6. quality of life, and 7. special
location needs. Findings suggested that not-for-profit associations attach
more importance to the appraisals of potential facilities, employee
factors, and available transportation than to the other attributes. No
organizational characteristics were identified that consistently
differentiated respondents' ratings of site attributes. However,
respondents with centralized offices did attach greater importance to
facilities in the decision-making process than did those with decentralized
operations. In addition, office building ownership made a significant
difference in how participants rated the costs of living attribute. Tables.
References.

143

Illustration 13.3—Continued

7/7/2
86018638
Location Decisions of High-Technology Firms: A Case Study
Jarboe, Kenan Patrick
Technovation (Netherlands)   v4n2   PP: 117-129   Apr 1986
AVAILABILITY: ABI/INFORM

Top managers from a sample of 46 high technology firms in the Ann Arbor, Michigan, area were surveyed about the factors that influenced their location decisions. Generally, these firms were small and of recent establishment and had high levels of professional-technical employment. Only a small portion of firms had been attracted from outside the Ann Arbor area; most firms had been founded by natives who did not investigate other potential locations. Local universities, workforce quality, quality of life, and transportation availability were listed as the most attractive features of Ann Arbor, while high local taxes and low availability of venture capital were considered the least attractive features. These results suggest that high technology firms do not emphasize the market access and operational cost-location criteria stressed by traditional manufacturing firms. Areas wanting to promote high technology development must stress availability of high-quality support facilities and area features that will improve firms' abilities to attract professional workers. Tables. References.

Illustration 13.3—Continued

7/7/5
85027190
DP Goes Suburban
Grosson, Robert M.
Datamation v3in15 PP: 22-28 Aug 1, 1985
AVAILABILITY: ABI/INFORM

Many companies are moving their data processing (DP) departments away from high-rent cities and are locating new facilities in the suburbs. Local governments in the suburbs are offering packages to attract DP managers that include: 1. low rents, 2. low taxes, 3. inexpensive power, 4. help in assembling tracts of land, and 5. ample single-floor space. Corporations are not moving their central headquarters out of the cities, but they are increasingly placing their expansion DP facilities and backup units in the suburbs. The right environment and quality of life that it affords are found to be important factors in obtaining and keeping DP personnel. There are certain barriers that companies face when making a decision to move out of the city. Banks, especially, are dependent upon a good business relationship with city and state governments. Although the movement to the suburbs is expected to be slow, it is expected to continue.

145

Illustration 13.3—Continued

7/7/10
84003021

Current Trends in Corporate Relocation
Roth, Stanton F.
Corporate Design v2n6 PP: 25-26 Nov/Dec 1983
AVAILABILITY: ABI/INFORM

A survey of companies in 35 cities revealed that issues of prime importance to corporate real estate executives are: 1. convenience of an operational location, 2. economic advantage of a location, and 3. quality of life in the corporate location under consideration. Other factors in site selection are obsolescence of existing premises, shifts in the availability of needed support services, and changing demographic patterns. Companies are finding the suburbs more attractive than ever for offices as a result of rapid escalation of rents in central business districts and less stringent building codes and cheaper land in the suburbs. Before a firm moves, a thorough relocation study should be made to identify and solve problems in such areas as: 1. resistance by the local community, 2. trauma of distant relocation, and 3. lack of social and cultural amenities. A wisely chosen move can improve the corporate image, lower occupancy and operating costs, and enhance expansion opportunities. Quality of life concerns are assuming more importance in relocation decisions.

Illustration 13.3—Continued

7/7/12
88023992
Selecting U.S. Sites: A Case Study of German and Japanese Firms
Chernotsky, Harry I.
Management International Review (Germany)   v23n2   PP: 45-55   1983
AVAILABILITY: ABI/INFORM

Prospective foreign investors must assess a variety of factors when reviewing the merits of operating in the US, and they must also determine the region, state, and locality within the US that is most responsive to their needs. This review presents the findings of a survey of 14 German and 7 Japanese companies operating in Charlotte/Mecklenburg, North Carolina, regarding the factors contributing to their decision to locate in that area. The overall priorities of German companies appear to differ from those of their Japanese counterparts, but in both cases, the decision is attributable largely to the community's: 1. accessibility to markets, 2. ability to provide transportation and freight-forwarding services, 3. productive labor force, and 4. desirable quality of life. For the German firms, the availability of support services and quality of the local environment take precedent over matters bearing directly on the costs of operating in the area, in contrast to the Japanese whose pronounced expense-related interests are affirmed by their close scrutiny of local operating costs and labor conditions. Tables. References.

Illustration 13.3—Continued

85003973

The Quest for High-Tech Plant Sites/How the States Chase High Tech

Anonymous

Chemical Week v135n24 PP: 68-74 Dec 12, 1984 CODEN: CHWKA9 ISSN:
0009-272X JRNL CODE: CEM

DOC TYPE: Journal Paper LANGUAGE: English LENGTH: 5 Pages

AVAILABILITY: ABI/INFORM

The main benefit of attracting high-technology industries lies in the
potential for new jobs, especially high paying ones. Yet, surveys reveal
that high tech is responsible for only some 15% of current US jobs, only
about 25% of which require any substantial knowledge of the technology.
According to a study group at the University of California at Berkeley,
high-tech plant site selections are not affected by: 1. high levels of
spending on education, 2. low utility rates, 3. low manufacturing wage
rates, 4. low unemployment, 5. mild climate, and 6. a wide range of
educational options. Factors having a positive effect on attracting
high-tech plants include a skilled labor force, access to airports, heavy
defense spending, and major universities. Negative factors include the
presence of major corporate headquarters and low pollution. Only 13 states
account for 71% of all high-tech plants and employment in the US. Most
states continue to work high tech. A recent Office of Technology Assessment
survey found 200 state and local economic development initiatives partly
aimed at high tech. The reason for such efforts is stiff competition for
the small number of plant relocations. Tables.

DESCRIPTORS: High technology; States; R&D; Economic development;
Programs; Site selection

CLASSIFICATION CODES: 8650 (CN=Electrical & electronics industries);
1120 (CN=Economic policy & planning)

?T 83032603/5

148

Illustration 13.3—Continued

83032603/5
83032603

Six Major Trends Affecting Site Selection Decisions to the Year 2000
Ellenis, Manny
Dun's Business Month v123n5 PP: 116-130 Nov 1983 CODEN: DURVAH
ISSN: 0279-3040 JRNL CODE: DMI
DOC TYPE: Journal Paper LANGUAGE: English LENGTH: 9 Pages
AVAILABILITY: ABI/INFORM

The widespread changes taking place in the US economy are making the task of selecting sites for new facilities much more complex. The changes will alter the basic rules for both corporate site selectors and economic developers. There are currently about 7,500 US development organizations spending large sums in order to attract new business investors. An examination is made of: 1. how a skilled labor shortage at a time of high unemployment affects the site selector, 2. how economic development organizations are responding to the high-technology revolution, 3. why traditional industries must not be overlooked, 4. why closed down military bases in the US make good private sector profit centers, 5. why foreign trade zones may help a business, and 6. how a company can profit from President Reagan's private enterprise approach to the Third World. References.
DESCRIPTORS: Site selection; Trends; Facilities planning; Economic development; Industrial development
CLASSIFICATION CODES: 2310 (CN=Planning); 1110 (CN=Economic conditions & forecasts)

2. *Quality of life* considerations, including easy availability of such amenities as educational opportunities, affordable housing, recreational facilities and environmental conditions.

This initial search also indicated that high tech is responsible for only some 15 percent of current U.S. jobs—and only about 25 percent of these require any substantial knowledge of the technology; moreover, desirable "non-high tech" firms (that is, those involving clean, high value-added operations) also tend to choose site locations in regions offering high quality of life in order to recruit high calibre professionals who otherwise are often not willing to relocate.

A First Quandary: What to Do about Quality of Life Issues

Some of these findings were rather suspect to certain commissioners and a heated debate took place as to whether or not "quality of life" issues even belonged on the agenda. The quandary was ultimately resolved by referring the issue to the MCEDC Steering Committee, which decided to at least continue the inquiry about quality of life issues, and to *then* decide what to do about what was found, the rationale being that neither regional economic development nor quality of life is possible to sustain without the other, although each may need to be promoted in a different way.

Search Two: Regional Planning Issues

Because information on emerging issues of concern to regional well-being is usually not available in published form except in major metropolitan complexes or other centers where such directed studies have been specially commissioned, the subcommittee felt that a "snowball survey" of experts (described in Chapter 2) would be the best method to use for identifying regional planning issues. They started with themselves and with the chairperson of the steering committee, and asked each and all subsequent informants three questions:

1. What do you see as the major *threats* to adequate economic development and quality of life in Mid City, especially those factors which must be anticipated rather than just reacted to if they are to be handled successfully?
2. What do you see as Mid City's principal *opportunities* for improving economic development and quality of life?
3. *Who else* would you recommend as being particularly able to speak knowledgeably about these issues?

Illustration 13.4 lists the types of persons who were interviewed, and Illustration 13.5 lists the types of issues which they identified. They are

Illustration 13.4
Types of Persons Nominated as "Snowball Survey" Informants in Search Two[1]

Round One

- The chairman of the MCEDC Steering Committee

- Each of the three initial members of the MCEDC Strategic Development Subcommittee

  - a planning analyst from a local corporation and a member of Chamber of Commerce Board of Directors

  - a political activist from a local civic organization

  - an educator interested in applied research

Round Two

- The executive director of the Mid City Chamber of Commerce

- The president of a local bank that is a leader in real estate development

- Two city council members active in zoning and infrastructure resource committees

- The president of the local League of Women Voters

- The president of the local Urban League

- A planning analyst with responsibility for regional affairs in the state government

Round Three

- The mayor of Mid City

- Four officials representing banks in Mid City, several of whom are highly involved in venture capital portfolio development

- Five real estate developers, three of whom are involved in collaborative regional development activities

- Three citizen activists, two from minority groups, one (who is also an educator) an environmentalist

- A powerful "behind the scenes" political advisor and lobbyist on developmental issues

---

[1] Each person listed in Round One was asked to nominate five persons. The researchers followed up on all persons who were nominated by two or more persons, or who were so obviously important that they shouldn't be missed. Precisely how many nominations each person got, and in which round, can be quite counterproductive to make known. This information is therefore not part of the scenario.

ordered by frequency of mention—an objective way of avoiding argument about the relative importance of issues which can be seen quite differently by people having different interests in mind. As you can see, only a few of the issues listed in Illustration 13.5 deal with opportunities as contrasted with problems, which although typical, does sometimes present problems for information research projects which are undertaken in the "real world."

A Second Quandary: What to Do Next

It was originally intended that the next phase of information gathering would focus on the three planning issues most frequently mentioned in the

Illustration 13.5
Illustrative Planning Issues Identified in Search Two

- Traffic density, especially at commuting hours
- Increasing unemployment and economic stagnation
- Escalating accident rate on highways and rising insurance costs
- Lack of coordinated planning among the municipalities, special districts, and vested interests in the regions
- Need for more green space and recreational facilities
- Citizen apathy and lack of civic participation
- Need for better access to Mid City's political process for minority representatives
- Decreasing adequacy and availability of water and supporting infrastructure
- Obsolescent curriculum and second-rate image of local institutions of higher education

snowball survey, and then, when appropriate, to also seek out particular models and practices that other regions had found useful for handling similar planning issues. The three planning issues of most concern in Mid City at the time were:

1. *Transportation.* Increasing traffic density, especially at peak commuting hours, the deteriorating quality of highways and escalating accident rate generally indicated that the whole question of transportation needed to be looked at anew.

2. *Water.* Decreasing reserve capacity of the local water supply, possible contamination of some local deep wells from industrial waste disposal and uncertain long-range availability from more distant sources made this the second most frequently mentioned issue by experts, although it was (unlike traffic congestion) virtually unknown as a problem by most laypersons in Mid City.

3. *Governance.* Lack of collaboration among different agencies, municipalities and interest groups in the greater Mid City region, although not most frequently mentioned, was the most strategic or pivotal of all such issues according to those most knowledgeable about Mid City. Specific issues frequently mentioned included transportation, water, environmental degradation and economic development.

In thinking about how best to explore these issues, the subcommittee thought that it should be reasonably easy to find research reports and other published information that describe forecasts and other *substantive* factors related to issues such as transportation and water. On the other hand, they knew that published information on specific plans "in the pipeline" on these issues, who is involved in different parts of the planning process, and other *procedural* factors related to these issues, would not likely exist—especially with regard to the third (and they felt, the most important) of the three issues—lack of regional collaboration. Nor could they expect to find in published form all that they needed to know about what approaches had worked well elsewhere.

Although the members of the Strategic Development Subcommittee agreed quite easily on the above points, they found it difficult to agree on what to do about them. In fact, the "group of three" got into their first extended argument at this point. It concerned how to proceed.

The teacher/graduate student who had become the group's information specialist wanted to push forward as rapidly as possible. She specifically suggested gathering as much future-oriented information about the above issues as possible for the commission to use, especially information on what had worked well in other cities. She was sure that when confronted with all of this information, the commissioners would have little choice but to act on it and take steps to improve the outlook for the region.

The lobbyist who had become the group's political bell-weather, on the other hand, argued for "counting the votes," so to speak, finding out more about how the major "influentials" of the community felt about these problems, especially the lack of regional collaboration. She said that she had too often seen political leaders back away from risky situations unless it was obvious to all that a true consensus for moving ahead exists, and that she didn't want the subcommittee to risk losing all that they had gained thus far by now trying to move too far and too fast. When dealing with the long-term future, she said, it doesn't make sense to win a battle but lose the war.

The real estate development analyst and chamber of commerce board member who usually fronted for the group had no strong position of her own in the matter, other than wanting the other two to agree. In order to find some basis for consensus, she discussed possible next steps at length with the Steering Committee, where even more views emerged—one of which was to back off entirely from "all this futures stuff." Meanwhile, many of the commissioners, including several members of the Steering Committee, were becoming increasingly uncomfortable about the growing impatience of metropolitan reporters for news releases on the findings of the commission, and how the media image of the city might suffer as a result of all this talk about quality of life problems in the absence of a clear-cut strategy for handling them.

Moreover, the few minorities represented in the MCEDC were beginning to vigorously press for more of a voice in the commission, particularly in its Steering Committee, and for more emphasis on "here and now" issues rather than those of the future. This also divided the Strategic Development Committee.

In the end a compromise was struck. It was decided to follow three different search strategies at once, but with different degrees of visibility:

1. For each of the three major planning issues, quietly determine the identity and position of significant "stakeholder" groups, together with the key "knowledge-

ables" and "influentials" associated with each; and to advise both the executive director of the MCEDC and the chairman of the Steering Committee as to specific persons who might be recruited as "issue champions" for each issue, as well as those needing to be informally lobbied before mounting any type of initiative to deal with that particular issue. Particularly emphasize the search for promising mechanisms which any group may wish to advance.

2. Identify a broad range of mechanisms and practices that other metropolitan regions had found useful in resolving similar planning issues to those which Mid City faced, and to make this information available to the Executive Director and Steering Committee as soon as possible.

3. Hold off, for the time being, with the gathering and discussion of more detailed substantive information on the three issues as a *formal* agenda of the MCEDC, but quietly intensify the search for information needed to prepare a "strategic outlook" briefing, closely holding this information within the Strategic Development Subcommittee until it is needed by the Executive Director, including whatever information on each of the three planning issues is deemed to be relevant. Meanwhile, the Executive Director and members of Steering Committee will assess the political feasibility of ideas generated by all three searches with the commissioners and other key "players" in Mid City, so as to fashion a workable consensus.

Searches Three and Four: Interest Groups by Planning Issue and by Power and Position

Although conceptually different, these two searches were done as essentially overlapping phases of the same basic process. In search three, an attempt was made to determine virtually all formal or informal groupings of people or organizations in Mid City, which had a vested interest in one or more of the three broad policy issues: transportation, water, collaborative regional governance. Naturally, much more priority was given to the identification of groups which are formally organized and an intentional part of the political process.

The method used was a simple one. The researchers started with selected Commissioners and other knowledgeable persons who were particularly helpful in Search Two, asking each the following four questions:

1. What organized groups or important points of view do you know of that have a particular interest in the "X" planning issue? (Where X was one of the three planning issues listed above, described in as much detail as required in each instance.)

2. What particular point of view, agenda, or specific initiatives do you know of that is supported by this group on this issue?

3. How much political power does this interest group now represent, relative to other interest groups which might want to exert influence on this issue? What is the main basis from which their power is derived? To what extent is their

power usually exercised in a "collaborative" as against a "turf territorial" manner?

4. Who else would you recommend that could give me informed answers to these questions? Specifically, who do you know in each of the groups you mentioned that might serve as a good spokesperson, not only for the group's position on the issue in question, but also as regards the possible openness of the group to forming coalitions with other groups concerned about the same issues?

Once a preliminary set of answers to the above questions was in hand for each of the three planning issues, work started in earnest to define the range of positions and the political power represented by each. The "behind the scenes political advisor and lobbyist" identified in Round Two of Search Two was recruited to help the Strategic Development Committee as a virtual task leader at this point. Among the insights he shared was the importance of distinguishing between positions which are taken primarily for the purpose of maintaining or increasing relative political power (i.e., "turf territoriality") as contrasted with those taken in order to get the issue resolved in a satisfactory way—and how each type of position can be appealed to in a different way for purposes of weaving political coalitions around a set of similar concerns. Not surprisingly, many of the positions held by different groups were found to be based on assumptions and premises that directly contradicted information being gathered by the Strategic Development Subcommittee in Search Six; but for reasons stated above, these were not pursued or discussed at this time.

Illustration 13.6 lists the types of interest groups which this search identified for each of the three issues. A "Groups by Power, Position and Issue" matrix, based on the results of both Search Three and Search Four was also constructed by the subcommittee, but it is much too complex for inclusion here. In some ways, an even more important outcome of these searches was the identification of potential "issue champions" among the interest groups—specific individuals likely to be willing and able to mobilize people in a way that would maximize, rather than minimize, the probability of success in weaving an effective coalition among groups having quite different positions.

Search Five: Exemplary Initiatives for Regional Development

Searches for published information on this topic using online databases turned out not to be particularly productive. But a combination of manual searching of different types of media, such as those listed in the previous chapter (Illustration 12.3), and a snowball survey of knowledgeable informants, particularly those in other cities where one or more innovative strategies were pioneered, turned up a variety of good ideas. A frequently useful source of "state of the art" approaches to regional problems turned

Illustration 13.6
Interest Groups Identified in Search Three

Issue Area One: <u>Transportation</u>

- The Mid City Committee for Public Transportation (a committee of the Mid City Urban League)

- The Mid City Transportation Committee (a committee of the Mid City Chamber of Commerce)

- The Regional Mobility Task Force (a coalition made up of representatives from all Chambers of Commerce in the Mid City region)

- Better roads for Mid State (an association of contractors and engineers who do highway work, and other interested parties)

Issue Area Two: <u>Water</u>

- The Mid City Municipal Utility District(s) (local not-for-profit agencies with statutory responsibility to provide water service in their district)

- The Association of Mid City Municipal Utility Districts (a special interest group which lobbies the state legislature for protection of regional rights)

- The Mid City Taskforce in Water Quality and Availability (a fact-finding and problem-solving committee established by the Mid City Chamber of Commerce to promote the adequacy of industrial water supplies)

- The Mid City Water Alliance (an association of regional water conservation organizers, drainage basin and river authorities, and engineers and contractors who serve these constituencies)

Issue Area Three: <u>Collaborative Governance</u>

- The Mid City Council of City Governments (an association which provides both technical assistance and lobby activities throughout Mid State.

- The Mid State Municipal League (an association of city councils and department heads which maintains a strong lobbying presence on behalf of small to medium-sized cities)

- The Mid City League of Women Voters (a civic organization dedicated to enhancement of the democratic process)

- The Intercity Conference of City Managers (a technical/professional group)

- The American Planning Association (a technical/professional group)

out to be URBAN LAND (published monthly by the Urban Land Institute, 1090 Vermont Ave., N.W., Washington, D.C. 20005).

Illustration 13.7 briefly summarizes the specific strategies that appeared most promising, both to the subcommittee and to the Steering Committee, such that they became principal recommendations for presentation to the entire commission.

Search Six: Strategic Outlook

This search is listed last in the series, not because it was done in that order or because it logically falls here, but because it proved easier to talk

Illustration 13.7
Illustrative Strategies Identified in Search Five

1. An Omnibus Economic Development Organization

Whether structured more as a governing council, a public sector foundation or a private sector corporation, many communities have found it effective to have a single umbrella organization through which to create, coordinate and promote many different initiatives such as those listed below. For more information, contact the AMERICAN ECONOMIC DEVELOPMENT COUNCIL (4849 N. Scott St., Suite 10, Schiller Park, IL 60176) or see the journal ECONOMIC DEVELOPMENT REVIEW.

2. The Negotiated Investment Strategy

With "investment" referring to the commitment of social as well as financial resources, "negotiated investment" is a process through which a skilled professional helps various organizations in the public, private and civic sectors of a region identify agenda in which they are clearly competitive; agenda in which they are whole-heartedly cooperative; and agenda in which negotiated cooperation rather than competition are agreed on. For more information, write the NEGOTIATED INVESTMENT STRATEGY PROGRAM (Charles F. Kettering Foundation, 200 Commons Road, Dayton OH 45459).

3. A Small Business Development Center

Funded by the U.S. Government and usually associated with a regional institution of higher education, an SBDC provides free counseling and low-cost training in all aspects of business start-up, such as business plan preparation, accounting and legal requirements, venture capital and other types of procurement. For more information, write the ASSOCIATION OF SMALL BUSINESS DEVELOPMENT CENTERS (1050 17th Street N.W., Suite 810, Washington DC 20036).

4. A Business Incubation Center

Offering direct service at low cost or for equity shares in the new venture, rather than giving free advice, the incubation center provides office space fully equipped with "pay what you use" services needed for start up, including venture capital, business plan development, legal, accounting, marketing, secretarial, photocopy and so forth. For more information write the NATIONAL BUSINESS INCUBATION ASSOCIATION (P.O. Box 882, Fairfax VA 22030).

5. A Support Group Organization

The Support Group is a national network of semi-autonomous organizations in various cities of the U.S. whose function is to provide low cost but high quality management training and consulting assistance to not-for-profit groups in their region. It defrays the cost of these services, principally by contributions from business corporations in the region. For information, contact The Support Group of Washington, 1410 Q Street N.W., Washington DC 20009.

6. A Loaned Executives Program

Executive talent loaned by business corporations on a temporary basis, or sometimes on a more extended "sabbatical" to public sector organizations in a region with special needs is how a number of regions have increased their capacity for dealing with emerging problems. A Loaned Executives Program acts as a clearinghouse for such exchanges. For more information on this and related initiatives developed by one community, write THE HOUSTON COMMITTEE FOR PRIVATE SECTOR INITIATIVES (P.O. Box 2511, Houston TX 77001).

7. Other Quality of Life Enhancing Initiatives

A wide variety of beneficial initiatives, most of which are not government-based, have worked well in various regions of the U.S. Those of particular interest to Yourtown included:

-Housing and Neighborhood Revitalization
-Child Care Community Planning, Resource & Referral
-Regional Resource Information Switchboard
-Environmental Protection and Conservation Coalition.

with community leaders about strategic implications of global issues only after their concerns about local and short-term issues had been addressed. In fact the "group of three" had begun their informal research ("before beginning") *both* at the global and the local level, so as to act in accordance with a dictum they ran across in the futures research literature: to "think globally and act locally."

As noted in the overview summary of all searches conducted in this project, Illustration 13.1, the purpose of this search was to *identify major trends, emerging trend reversals and other emerging issues and implications having strategic significance for regional leaders in Mid City.* In many ways, this search was the most interesting, but also most difficult for the subcommittee. Although they found it not at all hard to use the information search techniques introduced in this handbook to identify a whole range of exciting issues on whose outcome our collective future largely depends, the search techniques themselves offer little or no guidance in how to interpret the many different points of view offered by authors having different (and usually unstated) ideological persuasions; and how to appropriately reflect planetary problem issues when thinking about local planning and problem solving. Their task, therefore, soon became one of finding "intermediate syntheses" which would make their task a bit easier.

Ultimately, the subcommittee found the ongoing series of reports and books by two different U.S. based "global think tanks" to be more satisfactory than any sources of similar materials: The Worldwatch Institute (1776 Massachusetts Ave., N.W., Washington, D.C. 20036; and World Resources Institute (1735 New York Avenue, Washington, D.C. 20006; publication ordering address: Box 620, Holmes, Pa. 19043). From the subcommittee's point of view, the most appealing thing about these publications was the way in which they generally bridge the large gulf between empirical *indicators* of emerging global issues, and the making of reasonably feasible *policy recommendations* which tend to avoid the feeling of "gloom and doom." A summary volume by each is STATE OF THE WORLD, A WORLDWATCH INSTITUTE REPORT ON PROGRESS TOWARD A SUSTAINABLE SOCIETY (New York: Norton, a new version published annually); and WORLD ENOUGH AND TIME: SUCCESSFUL STRATEGIES FOR RESOURCE MANAGEMENT by R. Repetto (New Haven: Yale University Press, 1986.) Both groups have published penetrating analyses of water resource policies, both in the United States and abroad.

Although it is a considerably more difficult text to read, the subcommittee also found the following book to be quite useful because of the way in which it defines the major ideological points of view regarding planetary issues, and then analyzes these issues as seen by the different points of view: WORLD FUTURES: A CRITICAL ANALYSIS OF ALTERNATIVES by B. Hughes (Baltimore: The Johns Hopkins University Press, 1985). Finally, a book that offers both a highly readable series of "alternative futures" for

Illustration 13.8
Illustrative List of Global Planning Issues from Search Six

Key Obstacles to Sustainable Societies

- Population Growth
- Deforestation
- Soil Erosion
- Desertification
- Pollution
- Resource Depletion
- Starvation
- Militarization
- Economic Destabilization

Factors leading to a
decrease in the carrying
capacity of the planet

Key Transitions to Sustainable Societies

- A demographic transition to a stable world population

- An energy transition to an era in which energy is produced and used at high efficiency without aggravating other global problems

- A resource transition to reliance on nature's "income" and not depleting of its "capital"

- An economic transition to sustainable growth and a broader sharing of its benefits

- A political transition to a global bargain grounded in complementary objectives between North and South

the United States and suggestions on how to think about regional decision making with the future in mind: SEVEN TOMORROWS: TOWARD A VOLUNTARY HISTORY by P. Hawkin, J. Ogilvy, and P. Schwartz (New York: New American Library, 1982). The subcommittee even went so far as to photocopy the now out-of-print SEVEN TOMORROWS, so that they could give it to all of the commissioners of the MCEDC. Due to the serious, but gentle and low-key way in which this little book presents the likely future costs of *not* engaging in collaborative, future-oriented, regional problem solving, the subcommittee thought it a safe way to promote this message.

Because Search Six identified so many different types of global/national/ regional trends, trend reversals, and other emerging issues of significance, the subcommittee decided not to attempt a full reporting of them to the MCEDC. Instead they returned to *sustainable development* as a theme to focus on, but now at a planetary level.

Illustration 13.8 summarizes the global planning issues which were therefore emphasized in a "Strategic Outlook" briefing which the subcommittee prepared for presentation to the MCEDC. This briefing was seen by the subcommittee as a potential opportunity to make the fundamental point that although the list of issues in Illustration 13.8 may seem quite remote from the concerns of Mid City, they have important regional implications, such as rapidly changing employment base, unpredictable economic fluctuations and increasing international competition—all of which make long-range, collaborative regional development activities even more essential than they would otherwise be.

Organizing for Next Steps

It took less than three months of concentrated effort to conduct the six "searches" described above. Now the task became one of deciding what to present to the commissioners in order to maximize the likelihood that this "intelligence" would be put to effective use, rather than resisted in support of the status quo. Since the MCEDC was by design a temporary organization to get things moving, one clear task was to design a more permanent vehicle that would do just that, but in a sustainable way.

Due to their earlier success dealing with the sensitive issues described above, and because they had already identified the types of methods that would help Mid City become more proactive in its economic diversification agenda, it quickly fell upon the Strategic Development Subcommittee to draft one or more organizational designs, and to suggest a change management process through which they could be successfully implemented.

A first design decision was to suggest the creation of a private sector corporation, operating in the public interest and governed by a board of directors made up of carefully selected executives who represented the various key interest groups in Mid City, whose mission would be: the promotion of sustainable development and well-being in Mid City, and whose operational strategies might involve the implementation of initiatives such as those listed in Illustration 13.7. As the results of Search Five had shown, several communities had found that this type of "public/private initiative" offers a viable mechanism for both respecting a broad array of public concerns and yet having the ability to move quickly as things change. A second design decision was to recommend the name "Mid City Economic Development Corporation," thus preserving the initials MCEDC which had become commonly associated with the new type of thinking about the future.

A third decision was to put off until later the designing of the organizational structure of the new MCEDC (assuming that any top-notch chief executive officer would want to do this for himself), but planning in some detail that part of the new corporation which would have responsibility for continuing the work of the Strategic Development Subcommittee, so as to ensure that their work would be carried forward.

Illustration 13.9
A Generic Social Intelligence Architecture for Proactive Management

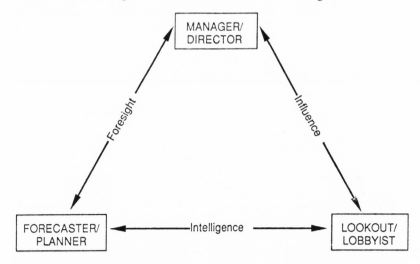

An organizational management consultant who had been instrumental in helping the MCEDC get past some of its earlier difficulties was asked to help work out the details of how this should be done. After interviewing key people in both the Steering Committee and the Strategic Development Subcommittee, he suggested an approach that was based both on the division of labor that had worked so effectively among the "group of three" whose efforts had stimulated the creation of this whole venture, and on the internal logic underlying the "strategic development methods" described in Chapter 12 (Illustration 12.9). The generic form of this *social intelligence architecture*, as it came to be called, is summarized in Illustration 13.9. (This phrase was chosen because the type of information the subcommittee eventually found was needed is that which is conventionally termed "intelligence." But to make clear the difference between this use of information research and classified intelligence methods used for national defense, the term "social" intelligence was used. Finally, as pointed out by a subcommittee member who is a specialist in computerized information systems, the term "architecture" has recently taken on a new meaning. In addition to "bricks and mortar" buildings, it often nowadays also refers to the organization of information systems involving specific types of hardware, software, and procedural management policies through which information is gathered, processed, and used. Hence the appellation "social intelligence architecture.")

Because of the way in which the MCEDC, to be successful, would need to involve "shared foresight" within not only its own body, but among a number of different organizational leaders in the region as well, two different

Illustration 13.10
Social Intelligence and Proactive Management within a Formal Organization

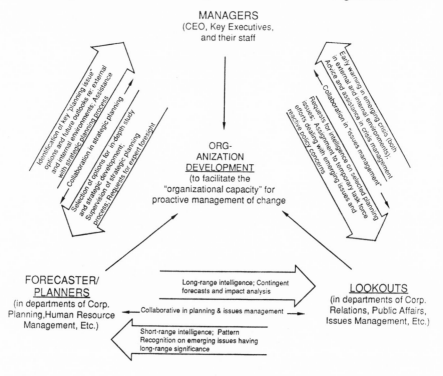

detailed designs of the "architecture" were worked out: Illustration 13.10 for envisioning how people can collaborate *within a specific organization*; and Illustration 13.11 for *collaboration of many organizations* having a common purpose. Although the subcommittee recognized that there might be resistance to formalizing this type of intelligence work within the MCEDC, they planned to overcome it by demonstrating what this type of approach had already accomplished thus far.

"Before Beginning Again"

Once the above recommendations had been decided on, only two major tasks remained for the Strategic Development Subcommittee to do:

1. Design a process through which most of the findings and all of the recommendations described above would be reported out to the commissioners for discussion and decision.

2. Assess the current status of each of the major tasks embodied in the Strategic

Illustration 13.11
Social Intelligence and Proactive Management within a Community or Network of Organizations

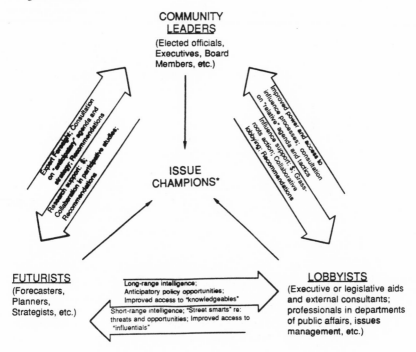

*Sometimes called a "networker" or "point man," the "issue champion" (like the "product champion" described by Peters and Waterman in *In Search of Excellence*) provides the legitimacy, inspiration, and coordination necessary for successful collaborative action.

Intelligence Cycle (described in Chapter 12 and displayed on the inside back cover of the handbook), so as to become clear about: (a) what had been accomplished as against what had been intended; (b) what new questions and tasks now appear important to pursue; and (c) which of these need to be done before the next major meeting of the commission, as against being put off as early agenda for the revised MCEDC (the "Corporation").

Remembering their earlier difficulties about the political sensitivity of information they collected, and recognizing that their main mission was now to help get a new and more permanent organization launched, the subcommittee asked the same management consultant who had helped the MCEDC several times previously to help with both of the above tasks. To their surprise, he made a bold suggestion. Rather than continue defensively keeping the essence of their approach and the intelligence they had collected under wraps, why not take the high ground and design a briefing that would do the following: Inspire the commission with a vision of what is possible, and then follow up quickly with a tough-minded presentation of how and why use of appropriate methods and tools should make a visionary approach to the future of Mid City feasible to implement?

Toward this end, the subcommittee prepared a "working briefing" for the Steering Committee and a few selected community leaders who were all considered to be reasonably "charismatic," which emphasized:

1. The main features of the Strategic Intelligence Cycle, and how it had been followed informally in doing the research that led to the creation of the commission, the statement of mission, and so forth;

2. How the Cycle had been adapted to meet the needs of the MCEDC and followed a second time as the six search projects described above were designed and conducted;

3. How Stages 4 and 5 of the Cycle (Select Strategies and Refine Information/Intelligence Needs) now needed to be thought through with the new MCEDC in mind, such that when the new corporation is begun, its key staff could be up to speed almost at once in support of its Chief Executive Officer and Board of Directors as they pursue the designated strategies.

One of the main accomplishments of the working session was the translation of academic-sounding phrases such as "shared foresight," "sustainable economic development," and "regional well-being" into meaningful political rhetoric, and a workable plan for communicating it.

The rest, as they say, is "future history."

14

Parting Tips

This chapter has been designed to help researchers avoid some common problems which can be very time-consuming, not to mention frustrating. In addition, it contains some important research hints. These tips are more often learned in the school of hard knocks and are frequently used only by professional researchers and information scientists. Specific tips on online searching are also included as well as some common searching mistakes that are often made by novice searchers.

INFORMATION AND THE FUTURE is designed to be used as a reference manual as well as a source on the theory of information retrieval. When it is read from front to back it leads the prospective researcher through the research process from beginning to end and explains the theory behind the process. Chapter 13, The Future of Economic Development and Quality of Life in Mid City: A Scenario, provides a kind of synopsis of the processes described earlier in the book as well as an example of how the book could be used. For the more experienced researcher the individual chapters in Part II, Sources, can serve as a reference for finding certain types of information or services. This handbook should be kept handy for consultation during the initial planning phase of an information search as well as during the adaptation phase.

Any Handbook Is Outdated by the Time It Goes to Press

While this is certainly true it is also true that the research principles outlined in this book are not out of date and will be useful for a long time to come. The reason that most handbooks become outdated is that the information about specific publications becomes incorrect. Many times a new edition is published. In other instances the publication listed in the handbook is supplanted by a different book or service. These circumstances are easily verified in almost any library using the bibliographic tools discussed in Part II of this handbook. The more general information about research techniques, search strategy, and intelligence gathering will remain useful long after the specific sources mentioned are obsolete. Research techniques themselves have not changed as much as the tools that are available to implement them. This book is not designed to be a researcher's only source of information and guidance but rather to be a guide to other sources and resources that are readily available in most locations. Reference librarians and other information specialists can be of great help for certain subjects not covered by this book or for more involved research activities.

It Is More Important to Learn How to Find Things Than to Memorize Specific Sources

The idea behind INFORMATION AND THE FUTURE is that researchers need to learn how to do research from a theoretical point of view. It is not enough to know where to find a certain fact for a specific project. The really competent researcher needs to know how to find a source for whatever facts are needed and how to translate those facts into situational intelligence. The tools and techniques in this book attempt to teach the methods and the theoretical base necessary to be a competent researcher.

The library's catalog, the various types of reference books and various services offered by the library and described in this book are much more valuable information than the knowledge that specific reference works exist.

People Are Sometimes Better Sources Than Databases

This is especially true when investigating the current status of a given topic, or information that is not likely to be published at all. Thus, personal communication with experts is often of vital importance. When considering such sources, it is important to assess your need for information through their eyes. This is done to ensure that you can communicate to them a valid rationale as to why they should spend their valuable time talking to you. THIS SOURCE OF INFORMATION SHOULD NOT BE MISUSED.

Adapt Rather Than Adopt

There are no rigid, exact formulas for retrieving and using information. INFORMATION AND THE FUTURE is intended to provide guidelines which can then be adapted to the situation rather than adopted verbatim.

Information research is an art, not a science, and searchers must learn to be flexible.

Don't Get in a Rut

This is actually a corollary to "Adapt rather than adopt." What is good in one situation may not be as suitable in another situation. Some researchers learn one technique or process and then attempt to apply it to every research project. This may work in a limited way but a more flexible approach to the problem is almost certain to yield better results.

Hard Copy Is Best at First

Online services are usually based on corresponding print products. This being the case, the more a researcher knows about the print version of the source, the easier it will be to use both the print and the online versions. Also, a quick perusal of the print version can save both money and online time. For instance, there may be many more citations on a topic than the searcher anticipated and the search can be redefined at the beginning of the process instead of halfway through.

Get Organized Before You Begin

Unfocused projects can waste incredible amounts of time and money. By planning a search strategy for an information search the researcher ensures that all facets of the project will be covered during the information retrieval process. Systematic information searching is an excellent way to save time and money and to be sure that the search is carefully planned and executed.

The More You Know about the Information Systems, the More Cogent Your Search or Request

Familiarity with an information retrieval system or bibliographic tool is useful to researchers whether or not they do their own database searching. Systems knowledge can help them frame questions in ways that make the most efficient use of the system, for both a researcher and a client.

The More You Know about What You Want Information for, the More Cogent Your Search or Request

At any stage of the information search process, decisions must be made about whether to broaden or to more tightly focus the search, whether to search more deeply or more superficially, and whether to seek out competing points of view in a given field, or to assume consensus. The more you know about why you are doing a given search, the easier it is to design an efficient search process, regardless of what information systems are used.

A Little Bit of Empathy in the Searcher-Client Relationship Goes a Long Way

A corollary of the two points discussed above is that if either the searcher or the client of information search services knows next to nothing about the needs and the concerns of the other, it is much more difficult to achieve a good result. An attitude of caring interest on both sides can significantly improve things, regardless of how sophisticated either may be.

Wygant's Law of Database Searching: Just Because You Can Doesn't Mean You Should

It is best to keep things simple and to not use the full power of the system if the researcher is not an experienced searcher. Many times an inexperienced searcher's retrieval contains some relevant information but not all of the relevant information available in the database.
Example: Don't use NOT to get rid of a set. (The NOT command exists in almost all the commercial search systems.)

Group 1	Group 2	Group 3
AA	AB	BB

A(desired set) and not B(undesired set) leaves only Group 1 because Group 2 and Group 3 both contain B. It would be better to say A—this will retrieve both Group 1 and Group 2.

Common Mistakes

Giving up too early or hanging on too long. Knowing when to quit is very important. The information gathering process is naturally cyclical and the researcher can become trapped in the cycle. There is almost always some more data to be gathered. The question is whether or not that data is worth the time and effort it will take to find it.

Not using controlled vocabulary when it's available. When indexes, abstracts, and online files are based on a specific set of vocabulary terms it is better to use those terms whenever possible. In many instances the assigned controlled vocabulary term will retrieve a relevant record even though the title or abstract makes no mention of the term. This is especially true when a concept has many synonyms.

Not writing everything down or not saving search printouts. Reference librarians are often called upon to provide missing information from a bibliographic citation or to identify the source of an unmarked photocopy. By keeping complete notes and saving all the paper generated by an information search the researcher will save a great deal of time and trouble.

Waiting too late to take advantage of interlibrary loan and other special services. Procrastination is the bane of research. Good information retrieval requires time enough to take advantage of all the services open to library patrons. Some of these services such as interlibrary loan and database searching services require several days or weeks to complete a transaction.

Use a Professional When Things Get Complicated

This is not just another chance to give reference librarians and other information professionals some good press. Some systems are so complex that they require the services of a professional. Information consumers are often unaware of how valuable it can be to have professional help, especially someone who is a frequent and efficient user of the systems, both print and manual. The astounding thing is that this professional help is frequently available free from reference librarians.

Information Technologies Are Not Value-Neutral. Use Them with Intelligence

Throughout this handbook we have tried to show how information relevant to many different purposes can be efficiently retrieved. In the scenario portrayed in the previous chapter we showed how, in some instances, more information is not necessarily better. People differ greatly in their views of how, when, and to whom different types of information should be made available, ignored, or suppressed. They differ as well regarding who should decide these things.

A premise underlying this entire book is that as increasingly powerful information technologies become available, it is important that all classes of people have access to them in ways that will facilitate—rather than inhibit— their effective use in the democratic process of pluralistic politics. This requires the use of intelligence in both senses of the word.

PART IV

APPENDIXES

APPENDIX I

Library of Congress Filing Rules

Card catalogs and library reference works are filed differently from the filing systems used by most businesses. With the advent of computer-generated catalogs some of the traditional filing rules are no longer observed but they are still useful in many instances such as when searching BOOKS IN PRINT.

This is not nearly a complete list of filing rules but rather a very general set of guidelines.

1. NOTHING COMES BEFORE SOMETHING. *Accent* comes before *accents; old* comes before *olden.*

2. ALPHABETICAL ARRANGEMENT IS WORD-BY-WORD RATHER THAN LETTER-BY-LETTER. Examples of word-by-word and letter-by-letter arrangement are:

WORD-BY-WORD	*LETTER-BY-LETTER*
Old Bailey	Old Bailey
Old Colony	Old Colony
Old Glory	Oldenburg
Old Hickory	Olden times
Old Ironsides	Older
Old Oaken Bucket	Old-fashioned
Old Testament	Old Glory
Olden times	Oldham
Oldenburg	Old Hickory
Older	Old Ironsides
Old-fashioned	Old Oaken Bucket
Oldham	Old Testament

3. ABBREVIATIONS ARE FILED AS IF THEY WERE SPELLED OUT: St. is filed saint, Mr. is filed Mister.

4. NAMES BEGINNING WITH MC AND M' ARE ARRANGED AS IF THEY WERE SPELLED MAC.

5. DEFINITE AND INDEFINITE ARTICLES AT THE BEGINNING OF TITLES AND OTHER HEADINGS ARE IGNORED.

6. HISTORICAL SUBHEADINGS ARE FILED IN CHRONOLOGICAL ORDER.

7. BOOKS BY A PERSON ARE FILED BEFORE BOOKS ABOUT THE SAME PERSON.

8. THE LATEST EDITION OF A BOOK IS FILED BEFORE THE EARLIER EDITIONS.

APPENDIX II

Annotated Bibliography on Database Searching

No other development in this century has increased the potential for user access to information to the degree that online database development has.

Louise Darling
in HANDBOOK OF MEDICAL LIBRARY PRACTICE. 4th ed. Volume I.
Chicago: Medical Library Association, 1982, p. 10.

Dewey, Patrick R. 1983. A Professional Librarian Looks at the Consumer Online Services... The Source, Compuserve, Apple Bulletin Board, *et al.* ONLINE 7:36–41.
  Describes and compares all the major information utilities and includes a bibliography and a directory of the utilities covered with their addresses.
Falk, Howard. 1984. The Source v. Compuserve. ONLINE REVIEW 8:214–224.
  Compares these two broad-based information utilities and offers suggestions for choosing between the two.
Feldman, Beverly. 1985. Database Directories: Review and Recent Developments, 1985. REFERENCE SERVICES REVIEW 13: 17–19.
  Reviews nine currently available directories of databases. Recommends the OMNI ONLINE DATABASE DIRECTORY (New York: Macmillan, 1983) as the best choice for end-users.
Harper, Laura G. 1981. A Comparative Review of BRS, DIALOG, and ORBIT. REFERENCE SERVICES REVIEW 9:39–51.
  Lengthy overview of database searching as well as a comparison of the three systems. Includes glossary and numerous illustrations.

Hewison, Nancy S. 1986. WILSONLINE. MEDICAL REFERENCE SERVICES QUARTERLY 5:81–90.

Provides an excellent summary of WILSONLINE services and databases.

Huleatt, Richard S. 1986. Bibles for Database Selection. ONLINE NEWSLETTER 7:3–4.

Short, concise articles which review three major database directories.

Humphrey, Susanne M., and Biagio, John Melloni. DATABASES: A PRIMER FOR RETRIEVING INFORMATION BY COMPUTER. Englewood Cliffs, N.J.: Reston, Prentice-Hall, 1986.

A primer designed to help the novice take advantage of computerized information retrieval services.

Janke, Richard V. 1983. BRS/After Dark: The Birth of Online Self-Service. ONLINE 7:12–29.

Extensive examination of this widely used service which compares it to other similar services available from other vendors.

————. 1985. Three New Online Directories: How They Measure Up. DATABASE 8:6–9.

Reviews three valuable database directories, all of which are excellent sources.

Lesko, Matthew. THE COMPUTER DATA AND DATABASE SOURCE BOOK. New York: Avon, 1984.

Provides capsule summaries of commercial and government databases and descriptions of public data sources as well as a section on how to use the Freedom of Information Act.

Levy, Louise R. 1984. Gateway Software: Is It for You? ONLINE 8:67–79.

Examines and critiques gateway software. Includes some excellent comparison charts and tables.

Ojala, Marydee. 1983. Knowledge Index: A Review. ONLINE 7:31–34.

Extensive examination of Knowledge Index which compares it to other similar systems available from other vendors.

O'Leary, Mick. 1986. DIALOG Business Connection: DIALOG for the End-User. ONLINE 10:15–24.

Describes DIALOG's new gateway system which provides unskilled searchers with access to DIALOG's business databases and services.

————. 1985. Gateway Software to the Information Stars. PC MAGAZINE 4:181–188.

Explains the gateway concept and describes and compares some of the services available.

Tenopir, Carol. 1984. Online Searching in the Popular Literature. LIBRARY JOURNAL 109:2242–2243.

A short bibliographic essay on online searching.

————. 1986. Why Don't More People Use Databases? LIBRARY JOURNAL 111:68–69.

Discusses some of the problems encountered by end-users and briefly outlines some solutions.

Weber, Jurgen. 1986. A Scientific Search for a Scientist. HEALTH CARE ONLINE 1:1–2.

Describes an online search for a scientist who would be able to fill a new position with a biotechnology company. A good example of an online search for experts.

Wible, Joseph G. 1986. Searching Made Easy: Front-End Systems for Medical Databases. MEDICAL REFERENCE SERVICES QUARTERLY 5:1–13. Discusses many of the currently available gateway systems, most of which are not exclusively medical.

Author Index

Subject Index

Title Index

About the Authors

ALICE CHAMBERS WYGANT is Project Director of the Substance Abuse Prevention Program at the University of Texas Medical Branch in Galveston, Texas. Prior to her present appointment she served as Information Management Coordinator at the Moody Medical Library in Galveston, Texas. She has published articles on literary topics and bibliographic instruction and was a regular columnist for the *Special Libraries Association Bulletin* (Texas chapter) for nine years.

O. W. MARKLEY is Associate Professor in the Studies of the Future Program, University of Houston at Clear Lake. He is co-author of *Changing Images of Man*, has published numerous articles and contributed chapters on psychology, educational planning, economics, and futures research. He is chairman of the Institute of Strategic Innovation, a firm consulting on the management of change.